GUARDING THE BORDER

SEBASTIAN BARKER

Guarding the Border

Selected Poems

London
ENITHARMON PRESS
1992

First published in 1992
by the Enitharmon Press
36 St George's Avenue
London N7 0HD

Distributed in the UK and Ireland
by Password (Books) Ltd.
23 New Mount Street
Manchester M4 4DE

Distributed in the USA
by Dufour Editions Inc.
PO Box 449, Chester Springs
Pennsylvania 19425

Text © Sebastian Barker 1992

ISBN 1 870612 76 0 (paper)
ISBN 1 870612 71 X (cloth edition, limited to
25 copies, signed and numbered by the author)

The text of *Guarding the Border* is set
in 10pt Ehrhardt by Bryan Williamson, Darwen
and printed by Antony Rowe Ltd, Chippenham.

For Miranda

"Me I will throw away"

ACKNOWLEDGEMENTS

Poems, Cygnet Press, 1974
The Dragon and the Lion, Quill Books, 1976
On the Rocks, Martin Brian & O'Keeffe, 1977
Epistles, Martin Brian & O'Keeffe, 1980
A Fire in the Rain, Martin Brian & O'Keeffe, 1982
A Nuclear Epiphany, Friday Night Fish Publications, 1984
Boom, Free Man's Press Editions, 1985
O Mother Heal Your Son, Martin Brian & O'Keeffe, 1986
Lines for My Unborn Son, Martin Brian & O'Keeffe, 1987

Contents

I LYRICS

    Tilty Mill *11*
    The Green Aphis *12*
    In Memory of Sally Ann *13*
    The Death of Barbara Mayo *14*
    The Risen Christ *16*
    Dawn in the Evening *17*
    A Little Song of the Earth (Mescalito) *18*
    Within Her Saintly Heart *19*
    From Profit, Loss *20*
    Thucydides Heard the Amputated Greeks in Chains *21*
    Benny *22*
    The Vanguard Angel *23*
    The Celtic Hawk *24*
    The Writer's House *25*
    Hungover in Henley *26*
    The War of Watch and Pen *27*
    The Summer Girls *28*
    Bluebells *29*
    Shockwaves *32*

II ADAPTATIONS

    Autumn Meditation *35*
    Man Holding a Wooden Balcony *38*
    Dreaming of Li Po *39*
    Lament by the Riverside *40*
    Visitation on the River Yangste *42*

III ADVERTISEMENT FOR ITSELF

    Thank God Poets Can't Spell *45*
    Yes, I Love Rattling On *46*
    Advertisement for Itself *47*
    The Walled Garden I *50*
    The Walled Garden II *52*

IV INCANTATIONS

  Break Sea, Break Earth *57*
  The Time of Ecclesiastes *58*
  Happy Handsome Eighteen *62*
  The Narrator *64*
  If We Weren't So Far Apart *68*
  The Politics of a Split Second *71*

V LOVE POEMS

  On the Rocks *75*
  A Love Song for Saint Valentine's Day *84*
  The Artist's Wife *85*
  O Woman of Christ. The Invitation. *86*
  The Corpus Christi of Womanhood *88*
  Before the Time of the Sundial *89*

VI NARRATIVES

  A Citizen in a Monastery in a Time of War *97*
  O Mother Heal Your Son *100*
  Lines for My Unborn Son *105*

VII THE IMPENETRABILITY OF SILENCE

  A Nuclear Epiphany *113*

I

Lyrics

Tilty Mill

Can I ever return again
   To where I can never go,
To the dark green woods by the fields
   Where the tall grasses grow?

Can I ever return again
   To the child I was before
When I lay by the rippling water
   And the dappled light on the shore?

For ever and ever amen
   I am delighting there
While the sun on the wooden wheel
   And the millstream arc through the air.

The Green Aphis

Who made the little aphis,
    The plump green fly,
Strong enough to walk beneath
    The tonnage of the sky?

Who made his bent and trembling legs,
    Gingerly and thin,
Withstand the onrush of creation
    Rushing down on him?

Who made his soft adhesive feet
    Tread with certainty
Along my gently shaking hand
    Unafraid of me?

A life of careful learning
    All men understand
Can teach me only that he moves
    At God's command.

In Memory of Sally Ann

Can a dripping oar
Subtend all earthly law?
Can reclining youth
Immould all forms of truth?
Can spring trees and river
Punt and pole forever
Like her eyes or wine
Forbid the spy of time?
O can my lovely dream
Be dead at twenty-one?

I hold that pole once more
Like Charon with his oar.
My fingers I dip in
Cool water like 5 sticks.
I roam her dazzling skin
As warm and soft as wax.
And holding her I hold
The end of all my world,
For she is dead and I
Am pitchforked through the sky.

The Death of Barbara Mayo

Alone and terrified
Barbara Mayo died
Murdered in a wood
Where elms and beeches stood
On a floor of leaves all brown
In the bright autumn.

On the over-hanging bough
A sparrow witnessed how;
The gnat and spider saw
What was never seen before
On this floor of leaves all brown
In the bright autumn.

The ivy clutched the oak
Which held the cawing rook,
The bracken waved its fronds
Like a crowd of angry hands
On this floor of leaves all brown
In the bright autumn.

A rabbit nibbled quickly
Then hopped behind a tree;
A slug in its surprise
Withdrew its frightened eyes,
On this floor of leaves all brown
In the bright autumn.

In the sky the sun
Still shone on everyone
But wept on her the rays
Of gold and useless praise
On this floor of leaves all brown
In the bright autumn.

The blue sky and the little
Lambwhite clouds were still
Above the wooded hill
Bellowing with her call
On this floor of leaves all brown
In the bright autumn.

A stream not far away
Red with blood this Sunday
Then mingled with the sound
Of bells and cars around
This floor of leaves all brown
In the bright autumn.

In a dream I had I saw
The shadow of death withdraw
Till her eyes were living stars
Beyond this crime of ours
On a floor of leaves all brown
In the bright autumn.

The Risen Christ

Could I in sorrow sing to move
    The eye-filled stone that hides my grave,
Or roll the circle flat and prove
    The straight line round in such a cave,

I think, my dear, the moon would cry
    And dip her fingers in the sea,
And cup a wave and wash each eye
    And search and search in vain for me.

Dawn in the Evening

When smoke hangs low in the room
    And the dog coughs on the floor
And the star-domed opal moon
    Shines for evermore,

I sit in a quiet house
    In the snow-blown countryside
Listening to my friends
    With nothing but love to hide:

Hidden like the trees
    Waving beside the lake
That web the sky and burn
    At dawn when all things wake.

A Little Song of the Earth (Mescalito)

To find the shoot or sapling there
    Toward the earth direct a prayer
That rotting apples leaves and rain
    May feed the root that feeds the brain.

The rolling worm is not unkind
    But holds more science than the mind
Transmogrifying dust and blood
    To food which gives the choice for good.

But if with earth you mix your pride
    Expect both it and you denied
For in the soil of too much reason
    The worm is like a ship in poison.

Fields become like seas of pain
    And men like those who fished in vain,
For every tool technique or skill
    Extends the reach of good or ill.

Within Her Saintly Heart
He Laid My Bloodred Wreath

The sea rolls up on the same old grinding stones.
    Hands behind their heads men smile at the ceiling.
Let the vine encoil with the passion flower again,
    O let the words be heard that take me from my pain.

The red ash glows, the damp logs hiss and spit.
    Faraway a pelican swallows a fish.
Tortured men suspect within their cells
    Truth is more than honour may endure.

Machine guns tap the calm blue morning air.
    A tree is felled. A robin dies in Spain.
Deep sea fish grow old and dim their lights.
    A panel-beater rests and wipes his forehead.

Brickwork breathes and moss ignites on tiles.
    This pain as old as fools rubs searching eyes:
Though truly believing I would love her through it all
    My curves of thought know no more graceful motion.

Between her ribs he walked, face to the ground.
    She called to him, 'Put out this burning doubt
And snuff the candle lighting his lonely stair'.
    Within her saintly heart he laid my bloodred wreath.

From Profit, Loss

From profit, loss; from loss, my heart of sorrow;
From time, my death, today and not tomorrow;
From hope, my pride; from pride, my downward fall;
From faith, my doubt; from love, my wounded soul;

From truth, my dark; from life, the sum of wrong;
From joy, despair, that lasts the whole year long;
From childhood, age, dreaming of all birth;
From birth, the pain that slowly turns to earth.

See how they smile; see both age and youth;
See how they interlock, and perish like a moth.
See the cruel eat, the gods of famine merry
Because they eat the wife, then child as though a cherry.

Forgive my words, forgive my heart of woe;
Where mercy is, is where we're not, but go.

Thucydides Heard the Amputated Greeks in Chains

Thucydides heard the amputated Greeks in chains
Weep, beating the Persian gold in workshed clatter,
But, to his honour, they, in the poor light,
Tongueless, noseless, legless, outwept his pity.
I see them, even now, the amputated Greeks in chains,
Choirlike, infused, beyond inquisitive steel.

Benny

How shall I, you so dead no dead were deader,
Black that leather jacket you creaked in your bed-sitter

On unmade bed and smoking, steel *Zippo*, *Players* and all
Books, and unwashed cups, and what the wed would call

The bachelor, unbashed, around you – (*J&B*) –
And there your love and there, I hope quite stoned, us three?

So summer shook and curled. Logs chopped on floorboards burnt
Red winter's hearth while we drank what drink we'd earnt.

You walked the moral round. None feared nor none respected
So much as poet-monks, when happier than neglected.

And wore your scholarship well, and wore your scholarship well,
No hinderance in heaven, and useful – eh? – in hell.

Then spring confusion gave. Where were you then, O Benny?
We saw you there in life. But you had all, not any.

The Vanguard Angel

In mercy of my means he stooped to speak,
    The vanguard angel of uncharted times,
And taught me how the earth itself will quake
    In firm adhesion to his chiselled rhymes.

He taught me how the angel of the poor,
    The angel of the junkie and of wine,
Stumbling on new space and time galore,
    Admit the wedge whose thin bit's not divine.

He taught me how the names of those we earn
    Like copper-plated letters in a hand,
Survive the concrete dirt we crowd to work
    Past Woolworths down the Monday morning Strand.

He taught me all the booing of the schools,
    The latitude the longitude to learn,
He taught me carborundum sparks the tools
    That slash the heads from idols as they burn.

The Celtic Hawk
(For Garech Browne and Gloria MacGowran)

Now in the honour of this deathless helm
  The Celtic hawk surveys the purple heather.
No hit of boot, nor sheep, shall overwhelm
  The iron sun that forged this world together.

I see a lake alaze in sparkling order,
  I see the sand-and-mica curve the shore,
I see the granite cliff shake on the water,
  And circles fish the surface by the score.

Before me, on the heather, drives the summer,
  Behind me, on the road, the cars of pain,
Beneath, the booming world (my heart's the drummer),
  Above, the blue of mercy stars again.

I was away and what I was was wonder,
  Wonder what My Wonder has to say:
But the lightning in her hair has feathered thunder
  That cracks her many miracles away.

For so we stood and watched that hawk before us.
  As brown as babies' arms it nursed the light.
We watched it claw the air before it tore us
  To terror's victims, flying through the night.

The Writer's House

Now in the winter of the Wiltshire hills
    The snow is flat and all the stars are bright.
The writer's house is quiet while he kills
    This vast damnation with his silent night.

The eyes of men, and shops of spinning wheels,
    Are shut, and slowly, through the jar of space,
He sees this planet, blue and white, conceals,
    Behind such beauty, hell in heaven's face.

And so, by minute, more to make amends
    With arch stupidity he might possess,
In hell he sees where heavenly conscience ends
    In heaven where hell is learning how to bless.

Hungover in Henley

Antique England sizzles in
    Coloured snapshots on the high.
Silver tongs and rolling pin
    Feed the proud nostalgic eye.

Copper kettle, feathered hat,
    Printed linen, jelly mould,
One-eighty-thou a freehold that
    Red dot indicates is sold.

Floury loaves, meringues, old wine,
    Cotton aprons, coffee shoppes,
Patchwork cushions, polished pine,
    And a glass jar of snowdrops.

Buttered muffins, flintwork church,
    Elizabethan timber-frames,
Higgledy graves, a dancing birch,
    And I'm in alcoholic flames.

The War of Watch and Pen

In pace with clockwork trotting round the face
My left wrist wears, my right and writing hand
Does jigger too. The war of watch and pen
Here meets in me the battlefield I've banned.

And so while stopwatch clicks the athlete's frame,
And fins of brass dial the graduate sun,
My watch keeps time by flashing out a world
My making pen denies, by making it, for one.

So tears descend, but only so in time.
Hitched to the pulse, so men and women think.
Drummers hammer rhythm, nailing time.
But all are still forever in a poet's ink.

Not arrogance, nor pride, nor vast Eternity
Sawing her 'cello in the Church of Space,
Make this possible, but facts I do not know
If pen is watch, watch pen, or zero, grace.

The Summer Girls

Whatever there was then, there's nothing now.
The summer girls have chased our spring away.
Aloud with light, there's nothing they can say
Who own no rival in their tribe's desire.
Whoever struck them, sparked off fire in fire,
And they are waiting shapely within this why and how.

The gutless rhetoric of conscience spewing
Would justify the sweetness of its lust,
But when we love, we love because we must.
And when I see her figure in my door
Or breathe the inhalation of what she's living for
I think on love and not its proud undoing.

I've had the push and widely does my mind
Dilate on horror, when, with limbs between,
I see two souls with one more born serene
Exactly in that instant when I blink alone.
And all this life and all this flesh and bone
Are what it's all about when love is so inclined.

And so I love her, rummage as I do
In logic then I no more care to know.
When hearts get broken, hell is where you go.
Yet I for one am certain love is more
Than rags-to-riches dazzling of the poor
Who recognise and welcome the lost rejected you.

The summer girls have chased our spring away
Because her flimsy cotton in the sea
Adheres to that which shapes the shapes to be.
The buttoned breast and once more trousered thigh
May clothe the form but not my ravished eye
Who comes to love though love comes not to stay.

Bluebells

I know I make a symbol
Of the foxglove on the wall.
It is because it knows you.
          – W.S. Graham

She had a place to go and went
Like spirit stepping from its case.
I saw her battered body spent
And nothing living in its place.
Unshaken by this cruel twist
She has a place to go and sing,
For she is forever there with us
Where bluebells come up in the spring.

In shaded dells where no one goes,
And valleys where the heron flies;
By hedges where the pale dogrose
And blackbirds countenance the skies;
In every speck of sun or dust
She has a place to be and sing,
For she is forever there with us
Where bluebells come up in the spring.

The river winding through the hills
Redeeming paradise on Earth;
The ecstasy of love which kills
The unborn child before its birth;
The atom's astronomic hiss:
Gave her two extremes to sing,
For she is forever there with us
Where bluebells come up in the spring.

A jaded parson walks the street,
The brazier by the tramp's defunct,
The blasted rows of houses reek
Of faeces where the rats have slunked;
Toddlers learn to take the piss,
And policemen on the gibbets swing,
Though she is forever there with us
Where bluebells come up in the spring.

The rich imprisoned by their wealth
(The poor imprisoned by it thrive)
Approach world politics with stealth
And murder while they're still alive.
It's hell on Earth. Injustice is.
And yet the poor may hear her sing,
For she is forever there with us
Where bluebells come up in the spring.

The creeping sly delinquent fool
Fashions music out of verse
And thinks he'll teach the ruling school
How much his harmonies are worth.
Untutored in the art of fuss
He hasn't taught his pain to sing,
Though she is forever there with us
Where bluebells come up in the spring.

The cloistered judge, bewigged and wise,
Drinking serenely on his own,
Has had enough of people's lies
And warms a heart as cold as stone.
The echoes fade of conscience, lust.
Off guard he hears a poet sing,
For she is forever there with us
Where bluebells come up in the spring.

The saint alone in blood and gore
Among the matrix of the time
Red-handed takes the pulse of war
And bandages the chests of pain.
The victims, living, take their place
Back where the bullets louder sing,
And she is forever there with us
When bluebells come up in the spring.

Shockwaves
(for Robert Nye)

O green and gracious Greece, in early May
I saw you young and walking on your way
Tender with flowers, taunting me in bars
I slipped between, detoxified, to be
The human philosophical vision
Of the blue sanctuary of the sea
And the iconostasis of the stars.

II

Adaptations

(After Tu Fu)

Autumn Meditations

I

Diamond dew rots maples.
Death rattles the mountain's throat.
Gloomy skies vaporize waves.
Low clouds shadow fields. My heart
Breaks for one marigold. Home
Ropes my thought like that rowboat.
Here, scissors shape people's warmth
As wash-mallets pound thick coats.

II

Sunset tints K'uie-chow. The North
Star beckons me to Changan.
Those shrieking apes cry my fate
My home home for a strange man.
Law's scented halls haunt the night.
Mountain turrets horn the land.
The moon shines ivy walls and
Flashes the river reed plumes.

III

Dawn pencils the mountain town
A riverside sundial.
Fishermen row home low boats.
Swallows skim a parting style.
Court critics, sacked, sweat envy –
Their scholarship eats exile.
Where are my friends from childhood?
Polished horse gild their jail.

IV

Changan's a bloody chessboard
Tonight, played for heads with hair.
New jokes torch the palaces
Where fresh-capped priests kneel at prayer.
Gongs, drums, march the northern pass.
West, horses, winged wheels, despair.
Here, fish slither cold snake lymph
And home, and peace, spell nightmare.

V

Mountains praise P'eng-lai Palace.
Wu's bronze columns drip with dew.
Night's lake recalls fleshless stars
Lao Tzu might wander through.
Feathered fans unfold the throne
Dragons prowl on silk, sky blue.
Death to wake up smelling fog,
Clutched by grief asleep and true.

VI

Autumn bronzes Chut-t'ang gorge.
The river mist bends for miles.
Leaves skate in the walled gardens.
Fresh news of war kills court smiles.
Yellow cranes and pearl inlaid,
Seagulls, masts, and tall carved poles
Freeze our past. The Prince kneels down,
The Palace chills, and, weeping, rules.

VII

K'un-ming Lake shorts time and Han
Heralds ruffle dreaming mind.
A girl weaves stone in moonlight.
A huge glazed fish swims the wind.
Blackeyed seeds dot clouded waves.
Ice strikes the red-eyed lotus blind.
Who but birds steers these cliffs, leaves
An old man fishing far behind?

VIII

K'un-wu road twines a river.
Red-topped mountains plumb the lake.
Parrots peck and drop their rice.
Green the phoenix branches shake.
Girls roam for coloured feathers.
Friends at evening drink and joke.
Joyous bristles sketch it but
White hairs weep and smudge each stroke.

Man Holding a Wooden Balcony

        It is autumn and the wind
                Shreds the high clouds.
The monkey's cries pierce the thin air.
Geese shudder over white sand
                Circling the island on the Yangste.

        Dry leaves swing to the ground
                Scraping the cold gravel.
The river like a tentacle of the sea
Shivers, scattering crizzled waves.
                Autumn abandons her sick companion,

        A man holding a wooden balcony.
                The river drags away
The last drop of a comforting dream
Long warmed in his temples now as white and chilly as frost.
                He must give up drinking wine.

Dreaming of Li Po

Brokenhearted by death, man's
Heart may yet heal; but love grows
Deeper with life shared apart.
Mists and waters each one knows
Shake neither free, nor a hand.
You walk my night. Night echoes.
Are you alive, ill, or dead?
I search through space, with no news.

I saw you walk through the woods.
The pass in the mountain snows
Took you from me. You were chained.
What use are wings, caged swallows?
I woke up and moonlight shone
The ceiling: your portrait froze
My heart. Waters rise with depth.
I dread your pain, red with blows.

II

Like bulls, clouds graze in the sky,
Heading to where they were born.
Will you ever return to your home?
For three nights now, until dawn,
I've dreamed of you. You were here,
As real as love, but more worn.
You rose in pain, remembering
The way you came: lakes in storm,

Rain, gales, hail, ice, sheet lightning,
The waves like claws, the sails torn,
Alone in a tiny boat.
Then, as you went, you, withdrawn,
Buried your face in your hands:
City gangsters rule by brawn.
Thorny comfort, the just fame
With ten thousand years to mourn.

Lament by the Riverside

"Old farmer of Shaoling
Sloping by the winding river,
From whom do you hide those small convulsions
Unsettling your chest on a spring day like this?"

"I hide them from the palace gates
Barred and rusting on the muddy river bank,
I hide them from the willow trees
And the green reeds."

"When last the Imperial Standards
Shook their colours in the gardens
Surely Chao-yang, our lady of the palace,
Winked at her lord in their lacquered carriage?"

"She winked because the palace gates
Flung open the gold of the evening light,
And she winked for the willow trees
And the green reeds."

"But surely all her ladies,
With bows and arrows, riding
White horses champing on golden bits,
Laughed when two birds dropped on a single arrow?"

"They laughed because the palace gates
Were huge and fortress to their frivolity,
And they laughed for the willow trees
And the green reeds."

"Such flashing teeth and eyes
Where are they now when ghosts
Are lost for shelter and the river
Weeps like a pilgrimage to the eastern sea?"

"They flash beyond the palace gates
Coiled and bound with green insurgent foliage,
And they flash within the willow trees
    And the green reeds."

    "It is early evening now.
    The horsemen return to the city,
    A dragon of dust smoking the sunset.
    When they bang, will you unlock your house?"

"I will contemplate these palace gates
Barred and rusting on the muddy river bank,
I will contemplate these willow trees
    And the green reeds."

Visitation on the River Yangste

A light wind combs the thin reeds.
The tall mast creaks and tilts slightly
Alone on the oily black of the moon-saddled Yangste.
Over the plain a glittering chandelier of stars
    Laughs, "Where is your name among the poets?
    Blown in the dust of the starless dark forever."

    Feet have grooved fame's rocky path
    The sick and hungry hedge with groans.
What happened to the smooth rhythm of my youthful feet?
And how is that gull circling between earth and night
    Croaking, "Where is your name among the poets?
    Blown in the dust of the starless dark forever."

III

Advertisement for Itself

Thank God Poets Can't Spell

Look, chums, we've had enough stick from the lot of you.
Lay off. And stop making those facetious, supposedly unnoticeable
Cracks about what ignorant pigs we really are.
If it wasn't for us there wouldn't be a language
For you to pet and maul in your drunken coddlings.
Behold! the poet is a man who makes mistakes
Deliberately, in order thereby to understand
The universal inability to cope
With the warm embraces of Mystical Energy –
Reaching out (I am terrified to say)
With irresistible ruling-class arms
To embrace her darling, her lost son
Weeping his amber gum
Under the outstretched cedar in the blue midday.
So, just to clear this matter up once and for all –
To outlast the clapping bells ringing us back
To boring existence – I say,
When a poet mis-spells a word
He respells it to the delight of scholars,
The pleasure of the intelligent among us,
And opens up the most delicious possibilities
For the unfading harmony skylarking in the spheres.
John Clare got it all right. The skill with language
Is fringed with heavenly luminosity.
And there is just no way your ugly stick
Can torture a screech confessing its birth in conspiracy.

Yes, I Love Rattling On

Yes, I love rattling on in metre unloved in the corner,
A big, doughy-eyed brunette clutching her pigskin dowry
Under the shivering chandelier across the polished parquet ballroom –
Or fluttering scarlet cheeks down in the wooden-floored
Town-hall cast-iron stoves stain red in the rafters.
For there I often courted her soft, her velvet forearms
Unnoticed in the rocking orgies of Dionysian music.
And so, just to spread it around, I offer this sound-proof number,
The just desert of my small conversation with her.

Advertisement for Itself

To intend to write poems is, of course, the first way to fail.
If, however, you don't intend to write them
They never get written. In that case, you may well ask,
How do they get written? The answer to this is quite simple.
They write themselves. Poems are so clever, you see,
They are able to do this. They can also roll on their backs
Laughing at pompous asses. Or get down on their knees
And scrub the kitchen floor the guests have trampled on
All night, swirling martinis, stubbing their butts in the breadbin.
Nothing is impossible to the poem. The trickiest problems –
Like how to fix the jets of a Solex carburettor
Or the world's moral impasse – to it are kid's stuff.
Trees crack and fall, the nests of crows explode
In horrible gales, but the poem, like the burning hoop
To the lion roaring through it, remains unmoved.
Small ants hide in the shadow of a trouserleg
Clutching their silly pieces of wood, but our bold hero's
Like Jack and the Beanstalk. A poem knows no limits.
This is not because it is stupid, but because
It cannot understand the elementary paradox
Of a limited universe. It resembles the scientist,
Philosopher, or logician. But unlike each of these
It cannot understand its own explications
Even long enough to hear them out. It is, in fact,
Pure ignorance masquerading as scripture – which obviously it can't be
Since this is the Word of God. It is, then,
The old voice, fresher than lilies, discoursing
To another, just the same. It's so new, I do believe,
Photographs only expose the last age of countless.
Critics, too, are baffled by why their own brains
Seem more the object of study than the subject in hand.
The poem, therefore, returns them every sympathy.
Children make bad readers because they can never get out of the stuff,
And old men grow deaf only in so far as it is unspoken.
Men on high cliffs at sunset find the subject appealing,
And tramps at the bottle have found it worthy of interest.
Policemen treat it with caution, and politicians
Sing it softly in padded bathrooms. Football players
Are bashful and leave it to their admirers,

While motorcyclists allow the odd little portion
Its place on the tailpipe. Shop-keepers don't stock it
But sing it in the evening, when farmers too
Attend the drunken Saturday. Small boys throw stones at it,
So pretty on the Sunday pond, to prove it durable, –
And long-haired girls, spaced-out on hashish,
Have been known to recite it (though rarely to me).
Dogs snore when they hear it, adding a base line,
And cats leap from high shelves, trapping a cushion –
Revealing its sense of fun. The tortured lip it,
And torturers dream of their infancy. Humming potters
Feel it between their fingers. The rower alone on the ocean
Imagines improbable wings the fish learns of the gull.
Poets can't remember what it is, except when they've had a drink
Or commissioned an essay. And postmen deliver it
When they come with a gentle heart wrapped up in white.
Jewellers dream of it, but fear its priceless touch,
And millionaires sell their homes (at the top of the snail's shell)
For something a little more lively. Actresses fluff it
Except alone in the bedroom with one they love,
And chartered accountants know exactly what it is
Enchanted to be surprised, pleased, or cared for
By those who are not their own. Business men grow wary
Sensing the ultimate rip-off, and ballerinas turn boring
Giddy on their flat feet, plotting their new conquests
They achieve without effort. Toads perform it,
Flicking over the duckpond the adhesive tongue,
And hungry kittens mewling on the doorstep
Are not much worse. Furious editors
Dictate it on occasions, but seldom on Sundays;
And finger-filing secretaries unleash it
Through tailored splits murdering married eyes.
Comedians are terrified of nothing
But what they can smell of it. Bankers
Get a bit loopy if they touch it in the crocus,
Tampering with demotion. Yet lovers ruin it
Just as often, greedy for the final wham-bam.
Drunks can't remember their lines, and heroin addicts
Can't remember anything else

Worth having back. Newts in the river enjoy it, –
And stags interlocking, thundering forehead to forehead,
Proudly display it. The man on the run rejects it,
A question of weight – and the man running after him holds it
In the glittering gun. Post Office clerks stamp it
On the face of John Keats, a true memorial,
O annus mirabilis, who did much the same in your life!
Lions snore it, noses ignoring the giant thighbone
Straggly with meat in the zoo cage childrens' candyfloss faces
Peruse the London noon. Gangsters pick it from their fingernails
And little miss nobody knocks it out on the midnight drums.
The Children of God have banned it with their iron cross,
And the Armies of Zarathustra shall march the earth in vain.
Ginsberg in California found it in his asshole,
For the fig, my dear, grows plump in the cooling orchard,
Red and juicy, slaking the amorous thirst.
And why should I, while my children skirmish with poverty,
Write any more, my inkwell as empty as my pocket?
Yet out of the hope that something may come in the end
Charging the lupin sky like the splitting of the glazier,
I toil on with cheerful ease, untrumped by disaster
Who to this very hour has sat beside me and sulked
Dripping my model of world with warm tears, dry blood
Clotting the golden curls. Small solace the horse-shoe wreath
Of fame. Trivial the backslaps. Damned rude the compliments
Alloyed with glycerine. Spurious the insults
Sideways on the pavement. For what I want is love,
And all your coy refusals waxen the darling boy
The tulip girl we all were and cannot be without it.

The Walled Garden I

Nothing will ever replace that small walled garden
Surrounded on four sides by the upslopes of pantiled roofing
Funnelling the blue sky till the air seemed shaking with
Mediterranean ideals. Along the southern wall
The purple eyes of the passion flower, ringed with white,
Preferred the passing sun to the dedicated sunbather
Brown on the green grass. For here we would devolve,
My wife and I, the terrible rigmaroles of married life
To nothing very simple, nothing complicated –
Just the passage of an afternoon, drinking orange juice
Under the fading parasol, while the unwanted sandwich
Curled at the edges, unnoticed by even the dog
Who hid in the shade, bearded muzzle pressed to the earth.
Below the tall and branching alder, the pool,
(Invented from an old iron trough), magnified
Our world around us. For there, glazed in the eye
By written brains, I would open the dustless lens
Of optical vision, and study the insects denting
The surface: in particular the waterboatman,
Who seemed as intent as I on the world below him.
The inverted snail, crawling the interface, drank
It appeared to me, our air as we his water,
Slaking colossal thirst along a belly of tongue
Till frailing tensions snapped, and he floated to the bottom.
Midget by comparison, the working elbows of mosquito
Larvae never ceased to amuse me, for to any
Slight hint of deadly life they scampered
Back to the depths, reappearing nervously alone
And then in confident numbers. The red goldfish
Fanned imperial gowns, each his own emperor
Or empress, dominating their world in which
They had one day been placed, much against their wills.
Yet how serene success had made them, slipping through
The bending leaves, snapping the offered breadcrumb
With no more thought than petulant gangsters, disgorging soon
As though something were wrong, then once again
Gobbling the lot and flapping on, rocking minute
Fiery-red spiders sleeping on the surface. The cool
Shadows touching without haste my shoulders warned

Such charming observations must, regretfully, terminate.
So rolling the grass to where the warm eiderdown
Still quilted my wife through clouds of speculation
Dizzy in sky and mind, I there embraced her
Calmly without desire, while under the peach tree
Whose first pink leaves tokened their adult glamour
Our six month baby slept on a crumpled blanket
Naked, the fine hair bleached both white and gold.

The Walled Garden II

Not long after the sun had sunk below
The western rooftop, draping the eastern corner
Where we came at evening, I would enter with glasses
Clinking on a tray, the tall wine corked and
Leaded, the Roman Vase – for those who like water –
Curvaceous at its side. And so by the patterned trellis
Whose greening boughs clematis and rose climbed
Freely round, cooling the glazed earthenware
Pots, we drew the corkscrew, popping the evening
Calm, conscious of the blackbirds, scruffy and loud
In all four corners – and our industrious sentinels.
Soon to our masculine company the ladies glided
Tipsy on kitchen sherry, balancing the heel
Unsteady on the soft grass – and trailing, as often
As not, long veils of white lace
Or, in glossy satin, taut on the silver bosom,
Flashing descending skies and every man.
Peaceful without music the conversation climbed
The echoless interludes. Candles faintly glowed,
Then englobed the leaning smoker, the air thick
With charge and counter-charge, merry as Olympus.
The pale moon thickened her deepening shades of pearl
Casting clear shadows where once the sun had been
Warming my very back beside the one
Now softly wooing my eyes from wine's temptation.
The yellow liquid tips from the autonomous bottle
Libating the five-inch-thick oak table
Plates and cigarettes, ice-cubes, and matches, strew.
The odd paper, clearly typed, half hidden
Under the forgotten glass whose owner strolls
The spongy lawn sucking the honeysuckle air –
Draws the inquisitive stranger who has not heard
The gifted voice of one who, prematurely,
Never reads a word, but counts it in the chambers
Of her heart, before the sound ascends and to that organ
Unrolls its tender way, and rolls it up again
Wherever it goes, so nothing is offended. Elspeth
Is her name, my father's wife, though not my mother.
And he, that man who some have quite obscurely

Imagined lives on air, not long after
Takes up the Sonnets of Gerard Manley Hopkins
And wrings them of his pain, till we all can see
The red wine blazing. The stars shake in the sky.
The earth tilts on her axis. The moon invades
Sane privacies with madmen's revelations. The shoes
Know the way and linking arms try bed.

IV

Incantations

Break Sea, Break Earth

Break sea, break earth, break clouds, break bread,
   break me, O hands,
I cannot bend, I do not bend, I break in hands, O hands,
Break me again, I turn to me, footsteps into forests,
   break me, O hands,
Break me, the sticks the stars make fire, I me, O hands,
Hands twist the meat, hold the bone, stroke the lip,
   untie the clothes,
Myself, O hands, you do not twist, I stand, I sit,
   I drink, I eat, I watch you hands,
I weep, you twist the meat, you break the sticks,
   you stoke the fire, untie the knots in hair,
O hands, twist break stroke untie me in this place,
   this night, this world, this me,
O hands untie me,
Break sea, break earth, break clouds, break me in sticks,
In stars, in flames, in flesh, your fingers,
Hands, wake me till I wake hands, wake feet,
   wake nails, wake lips,
Wake I, I wake in hands, O hands of thine.

The Time of Ecclesiastes
(For Sheila McIlwraith and Su Lynas)

For there is a time for living, and there is a time for leaving it alone.
There is a time for making love, and there is a time for love to be unmade.
There is a time for swimming, and there is a time for walking up mountain paths to arrive at monastery wells.
There is a time for refraining from striking a match, and there is a time for accepting a box of matches from a stranger.
There is a time for turning around and saying, 'Hullo, yes I will', and there is a time for turning around and saying, 'No thank you, I'd rather not.'
There is a time for Origin of Species, and there is a time for Consummation of Species.
There is a time for the conception of the individual person, and there is a time for the astrologer to mark as the turning-point in a calculation.
There is a time for the encasing of new computers in plastic, and there is a time for adding up numbers in idle amusement.
There is a time for looks in eyes to give rise to birth, and there is a time for birth to give rise to eyes with looks in them.
There is a time for belief in atheism, and there is a time for belief in abelief.
There is a time for Dachau and Belsen, and there is a time for Moral Parity and Christ.
There is a time for Hiroshima and Nagasaki, and there is a time for the Big Bang theories of cosmology.
There is a time for diving into cold water, and there is a time for withdrawing steaming cakes from an oven.
There is a time for running along political walls, trying not to fall off the political line, and there is a time for drawing curved lines, trying not to fall off the walls of physics.
There is a time for lowering the fingernail through the telephone directory to ascertain a particular number, and there is a time for recollecting a lifetime in a moment.
There is a time for observing cancer cells on a microscopic slide, and there is a time to remember there is nothing to remember.
There is a time for going to sleep, and there is a time for being unaware of going to sleep.
There is a time for imagination to flower, and there is a time, on the lapsed photographic plate for example, for the flower to imagine.
There is a time for great men, and there is a time for evil genius.

There is a time for abstract men, and there is a time for the feminine touch.
There are times when we wish there were no times, and there are times 'But David you mean to say you believe in God?' 'But Granny I'm not clever enough to believe in anything else.'
There are times when interest wanes in the cadaver, and there are times when the way out of life is simpler than a door.
There are times of course, and there are times don't be so bloody silly.
There are times when ladies and gentlemen walk across Waterloo Bridge in the evening, and there are times when bulls kick up their backlegs and leap into the bullring.
There are times for falling in love, and there are times for falling over in Underground trains.
There are times when astronomers are merely looking at other astronomers, and there are times when artists walk in the world in the flesh of astronomers.
There are times for Unidentified Flying Objects, and there is time for Uncharted Local Groups.
There are times for NORTON'S STAR ATLAS, and there are times for walking out into the back garden to look up at the stars.
There are times for entering and leaving time (even as a historian enters and leaves an epoch by taking down and replacing a book on a library shelf), and there are times for leaving time well alone and constructing dials, calibrating clocks, and paying furious attention to the engineering of wheel-balances.
There are times for knowing the whole subject (whatever it is) is a waste of time, rubbish, rubbish, and there are times for the recognition of the subject (whatever it is) because, like love, it remains unaltered.
There are times for approaching young girls with ribbons in their hair, to ask them the time, and there are times when money departs from a young girl's life like the wild ducks beyond a winter moon.
There are times when it seems like a good idea to light a fire, and there are times when it is most definitely not a good idea to reach out and touch a hand.
There are times when fat cheques grow thin in the monthly rat-race, and there are times when hills sink into the sea and volcanoes spill real estate into the ocean.
There are times when water wets the baptismal fount, and there are times when dust settles on a dozing marble mason.
There are times when glue won't stick, nor the kettle boil, and there are

times when the feet of marching armies shall never reach the ground.

There are times when the telescopes of the astronomer, and all the circles and quadrants of the astrologer, operate in reverse, and there are times when Nothing stares back, and No One can be understood.

There are times when guitarists dive into the sea, clutching their guitars, and there are times when chandeliers tinkle in churches an earthquake excitement of prisms.

There are times when prose won't do, poetry fails, prophecy repeats, and vision blinks, and there are times when the graduations of chronometry melt in atomic heat.

There are times when the myth of creation walks in the annals of God, and there are times when there is no God nor was there anything ever created.

There are times when stories do not begin; nor strangers absent-mindedly wander into a life, and there are times when deadly enemies walk up the garden path towards the front door.

There are times when panicking women etch copperplate handwriting with never a tremble, and there are times when secrets are revealed to a friend as to the reception of a kind of thundering uninterest.

There are times when a person wonders, 'What is the purpose of knowing so little about so much?', and there are times when the body of knowledge obscures the nakedness of wisdom.

There are times when the connection between time, and its grandest manifestation in the astronomical clock of the stars, eludes even the sharpest minds, and there are times when astronomy is to be adored for the dustless image it gives of the involvement in movement the Pythagoreans saw was also musical.

There are times when to understand the purpose of astronomy, it is necessary to understand that it does not have a purpose, and there are times when to understand the purpose of astronomy it is necessary to understand the almost superhuman responsibility that is placed upon its shoulders.

There are times when Governments order the elaboration of calendars, and there are times when chaps called astronomers are given the impossible task of dividing up the indivisible face of time, losing face, getting beheaded, and suffering the mockery of their wives, when they fail.

There are times when the central insolubility of every calendar is revealed to be the fact that the earth, the moon, and the sun, do not move a whole number of times about each other, and there are times when mathematicians seek the answer to the awkward fraction in Einstein's protruding tongue.

There are times when travel agents take down their appointment books from the wall, trains run harmoniously, Popes can seem to be minutely and accurately concerned with the things of this world, the holidays of secretaries coincide with the cruises of Italian dreamboats, the typesetters at newspaper factories glance at their Pirelli calendars, mothers have their day, and birthdays are commemorated; and there are times when the Angel of the Annunciation is precisioned within the armillery sphere and the orrery.

There are times when Christ Himself is born on His deathday, and there are times when the employee's grins at calendar factories annually have something to be proud about.

There are times when beautiful ladies will not rush from hotel bedrooms without calendars in their suitcases, and there are times when the sliest of monks slip the things into their baggage-of-retreat.

Happy Handsome Eighteen
Rend the books, lest your heart be rent asunder

Once upon a time in the morning, there was a young man – handsome, eighteen – and he was walking in the city.

He saw in a café a woman as beautiful as Helen; and she was selling coffee. He passed on.

The streets were paved with literature, classics lay in the gutter. He passed on.

His brain was rich intelligence; keen.

He passed a girl, her hair curling like commas and all burning-glory in one glaring eye. He passed on, O the world knows.

There was no time in the city; all time was in small worlds of eyeball. He passed on.

He who was eighteen saw in a window the bald head of a model, and she was. He prayed to God. Green tinsel wrinkled by her feet.

He passed on.

O city, he murmured, how do I look? And in the door of a glass block of offices, he grinned, O happy handsome eighteen.

On the greengold throat of a pigeon looping Nelson's column, the day shone. The sky, London, the world, flashed there like enamel.

He walked.

As the day lay under the night, the sunset made brief elemental love. In a room he lay on a mattress.

Naked thereon with a ceiling to witness he unpeeled his skull. Fingers of light ate like an orange his brain. No hour but now in the how is it possible present was the time.

He was born in the morning, his eyes as wide as lichees. The skin on his face was taut, as taut as a deathmask. Where had he been, what had he seen, where was he now?

In the drift of a seagull, close over Tilbury, the questions faded.

And so he arose and dressed and went to the bathroom. In cold water he rinsed his face.

Later in the day, he was walking in Berwick Street. What were you doing last night? he said to himself. A whore leaned from a doorway, smiled, and so he knew.

The Narrator

1.

I am the one who puts the song to sound.
I am the one who threads the eye of sense.
I tell the story. I put the thing together.
I am THE NARRATOR.

I am not the author.
I am not the person with a name.
I would have invented him, but he said
There is no virtue in existence,
I will go the way of my kind.
I am not always male.
I am not always female.
I am THE NARRATOR.

I have no interest in human life
Nor in the passing of generations.
They are interested in me.
I am not the human soul.
I am THE NARRATOR.

2.

I am the first sound of another world.
I am a rhythm, nor do I ever duplicate myself.
I am broken glass shining in the sun.
I am the singeing of the mind in the fire of pure reason.
I cannot be confused with the one who owns the copyright, dead or living.
I am not yet settled in a mould. I quiver. I am the light fashion feels in its head, just about to invent itself.
I glitter without let-up. I do not fade. I am the pulsation of the caesium atom: time measures itself by such a pulse, forsaking the archaic motions of the stars.
For as long as there is communication, I am among it.
I do not need to go to sleep.

I am at home in the wire room of the newspaper factory, where the sheets of news are torn off as they enter.
I do not have to face the extinction of the personality.
I have not lost my way, nor do I struggle with a memory of mystical matters.
I do not plot and scheme to get back to God.
I have never fallen from the mantlepiece.
I am not in need of fuel, nor do I run on bank-accounts.
I do not suffer from hangovers, nor do I have a guilty conscience.
I rise with the morning. I fly with the early jet.
I am THE NARRATOR.
I make up thrillers. I ravel, I unravel them. I write them out like making a piece of knitting.
Intrigue comes easily to me, it likes me, it takes me by the hand. I am honoured, but I am not falsely modest. I know what I am. I know what I have done.
I explore evil, as good, and both to their uttermost limits.
I am THE NARRATOR. I have heard the voices. I have listened to the reporters. I have met the eye witnesses. How long shall I be THE AUDITOR? How long must I be THE JUDGE in the court of my own making? Why am I afraid to rise beyond knowledge? Why am I afraid to speak?
Everything that has ever been told is what I have done.
I am the sensation of rapture in the penetration of a word.
I am the expansion of the dithering personality to the size of understanding.
I am a procession of logical sentences in pursuit of the wisdom of ancestry.

3.

I will not be constrained by the interlocking mentalities of the intellectual masons,
Who wouldn't know a kiss on the gob if they got one,
Getting lost as they do in the pocket calculator,
Whose circuits are the ecstasy of copper and whose microchips
Are telescopes to Eden.

For I am the logic of the lift-shaft graffitti. I understand the disgust. For what am I doing in a public lift, which stinks of urine, where shaving cream drips off the ceiling? Why must I pass through this indignity to enter the town in which I live?

Nor will I attribute evil to anyone.

For though it is bestial to be treated like cattle. And though it is undignified to be bombarded by graffitti. (Even as car doors slam, and the negotiating eye feels its way through the dark concrete corridors to the filthy staircases and lift-shafts of Car Park 4 in Bracknell). And though it is humiliating to pay for this experience by slotting silver coins into an unattended machine. Finally these states are stages in a journey. I characterise these states. I apply Guinness to their lips. Aspirin to their foreheads.

And I will be found at peace in the city Car Parks, weighing benefit against inconvenience, public opinion against private banality. For I understand the virtues of parking tax and the mischiefs of turnstiles.

Nor will I attribute evil to anyone.

For evil is the fearsomeness of God.

Nor is there a poison so roundly noxious, so rapidly infectious, so ruthlessly dangerous.

And nor is evil detached from the claws of God, Who needs His claws to get around inside the imaginations of men and women.

And nor is there a place in the imaginations of men and women to hide from evil, for the claws of God are winklepickers, and they winkle out the human soul, aghast against its background of no background at all, swivelling on zero, plucked out.

For evil is the approach of God, He has His styles.

Hell is a suburb under a claw of a foot of God.

For I am the logic, the fingers of butter, withdrawing the Mystical from the Momentous.

I am THE NARRATOR.

I was in the white heat.

I saw the white metals of souls in hell, clamourous, waving, shouting out the hot impracticals of pursuing a life of crime.

I saw the molten interior of God, brass-clawed with evil.

I saw the infinite universe of stars shrink before the arising of this power, the molten interior of God, brass-clawed with evil.

I sought men who work metals.

I sought men who work machines..

I sought men who can talk to a lathe.

I thought, If I can talk to a man, who can talk to a lathe, which can shape metal, which makes the machines, which make the machines which work the metals, then I can talk to metal.

And so I imagined God as metal, melted down, molten in the interior, yet so imagined, that as a mind moved away from the centre, it perceived the lesser metals ministrating to the centre, and so on outwardly, till the outward shape was glanced, brass-clawed, animate, moving, stealthier than the imagination which imagined it, God as Metal, molten in the interior, shaping Himself so as to instruct THE NARRATOR in terror, padding slowly forward, poisonous fumes rising like mist from every step, His magnificence unimpeachable, His dangerousness uncontainable, His glorious haughty dignity undeflateable, His beauty unassailable, His intelligence unimaginable, His power unlimited, His wit awesome, His generosity to frailty infinite, His authority authentic.

And so I began to love as fear ended.

If We Weren't So Far Apart
We Wouldn't Need to Communicate

If we weren't so far apart we wouldn't need to communicate.
The poet works in the communications industry on the rock bottom of the shop floor.
He works in words which are so much everybody's property, the very idea he might have a proper job working with such things, is universally held to be ridiculous.
He cannot make any claims with his words, because his words are just words, and belong to everyone, like pebbles on the beach or oxygen molecules.
Honoured or not, the extreme difficulty of his job remains the same.
Language is just not a plaything.
It both wants to stay as it is, arch conservative, and it wants to play word games with people's lives, arch revolutionary.
It sets up immortal changeless laws, like Spelling, Semantics, Idiom, Grammar, then dashes these worthless gods to pieces when it discovers the latest advances in Metaphysics or the Popcorn Advertising Industry have made them look futile and silly.
Many are called, but few take up the call: this translation of the ancient saying places the emphasis where it rightly belongs, for ultimately the vocation of poet, like the vocation of nurse or priest or saint, is an act of following through a decision.
The poet is singled out by his passion for creation. He is entirely on the side of the angels. His angels, however, are the kind that create devils just to keep themselves company. And so on through to the entire firmament of God.
All words remain to him infinitely fascinating, because he hasn't quite caught the meaning of any.
He studies the dictionary with groupie-like devotion, but he is not so daft he believes what he reads there.
(It's just jolly convenient to know what other people think).
He goes along with this consensus, and reveres it, but he struggles, as though with *machete*, to get through to the other side.
He is not the slave and tool, but the saviour of language.
His job is to get through to the other side to that place before language existed.
He must use himself as the crucible in which the fire of life and unforged language first meet, then commingle, then settle out to brittle words.
He works like a blacksmith, but where a blacksmith uses fire, metal,

and hammer, he uses fire, white- or red-hot language, and the blows and bellows of experience.

He sharpens wits, by revealing to them there are no premises for language to inhabit.

Language, personified as The Muse, is not so unconscious She lives in a mansion made by an Italian architect. She lives, if anywhere, in the tiny nerve endings and chemical synapses of the physical human brain.

She is tantalisingly close to Reason, but just far enough away to keep Her distance and Its admiration.

Her skirts flutter over membrane and mitochondrion, nucleic acid and subatomic particle.

She will not be housed by that which is Herself, language, yet She alone, like the coral to the Great Barrier Reef, is the life force of which it is the echo.

She is good enough to allow anybody to imagine he or she has invented Her, just as, everyday, the waving edges of Her skirts are seen leaving in dreams, love letters, and famous last words hauntingly.

The poet may imagine he is interested in, say, the objective nature of human sexuality, but this does not prevent Her from so softening his words that they sound like the consistency of cowshit.

He invokes her: She is out. He invokes Her again: She is out again. And so his life is an invocation, a pilgrimage to Her absence.

She is not in the least worried by all this, and counts it as nothing if She cannot remember where She left him trailing in the Universe.

He invokes Her again: She is out. His cry fills the Universe, but She is busy. At length, to shut him up, She simulates Herself and fobs him off with a dud.

The sensation of inspiration by Her descends to the level of orgasm, but it is never so two-sided and always more surprising.

A poet may approach Her the way a man or a woman approaches lust, yet She is always as sweet as the best of it and never has any throw-back.

The best things in life turn out to be Her service, those few poor words we said in a moment of gold, yet we dessicate and wizen in anthropoid humbleness, because She has not taught Her servants how to speak to each other nor to value their conversation.

(Communion with others we'll take – if someone else does the ceremony – but as for going out into the streets and seeking it there, Why, hell, that's too much like hard work).

She is the Perfect Personality, that's what language is, Whose perfect expression we call Poetry. Rather than re-enter a familiar personality, we would all much rather be living in that one.

She is the thing meaning was before it came into our heads.

She is the unformed, articulate.

She is the Bracknell of my imagination, even as Bracknell is the Bracknell of Her imagination.

She cannot be imagined without an image, nor felt without a feeling, nor can She be touched without touching back in return.

She is the ruthless idiocy of selfish mindlessness in pursuit of an evil passion, even as She sloughs off all destinations, burning in the stars of Unheard Quarters.

She is not oppressed by good or evil, for She knows nothing, existing both before and after knowledge, but not in it.

The Politics of a Split Second

Serious children walk darkness to school while envious professors spit out obscenities at rivals,
Sober voters slot crosses in churches while drunken ministers buy boundary lines in nightclubs,
Drawing-rooms glitter with crystal glass while truncheons beat skin the colour of blood,
Bibles thud from the presses while shoulder-held rockets of moral majorities roar through the walls of family planning clinics,
Men of God light up the world while the logic of devotion bombs the sanctuaries of the unenlightened:
Sorrow, drunkeness, and death kill my mind
But murder cannot move the peace which comes with love.

Theologians cross-reference in monasteries while state leaders sign war chants in high-rise palaces,
Sisters of compassion bandage ankles in camp sites while warehouses of high explosives take to the air in jets,
Wheat, butter, and meat mountain in plenty while bones crawl across sand clasping the mirage of an aeroplane,
Gold pours into moulds while beggars obliterate in a thought,
Heads of State promise fidelity while battledressed soldiers leap from their jeeps bayonetting sleeping relatives:
Sorrow, drunkeness, and death kill my mind
But murder cannot move the peace which comes with love.

V

Love Poems

On the Rocks

PROLOGUE

The nature of nicotine is despair.
The nature of alcohol is relief.
The nature of my love for you is air
And flesh. Your gratitude is grief.
I loved you in the kitchen and the public house.
I loved you on my knees and in manly sweat.
I loved you in summer, winter and autumn. But the applause
Of spring, no, never, not the great,
Great passion. Not the intense and mutual satisfaction,
The realized uncommonplace, the furious deliverance,
The heart on heart, the sum of each painful reflection
Jubilant in physical touch. The absence of presence,
The marriage of adoring minds. None of this, none of this.
Nothing but the social and adventurous kiss.

I

The first days of spring uncoil the tangled sweetness
We all know far too much about and absolutely nothing.
The ash trees clatter. The scattering-of-daffodils impress.
The birds seem to have no knowledge of the heavy and thudding
Gravel mills, the steel trains, the agricultural machinery.
Your return to my life like burning asphalt somehow caught
Up in my upper abdomen. In truth it's just the bloody
Heart clammering for attention. The shadowed thought
Of spring really does give me hope – not for your imminent return
(I couldn't take that) but for the principle of acceptable love
Returning in abundance the pairs and couples, the firm
Adhesion of figure-eighting dragonflies, the colossal heave
Of twenty thousand starry-eyed frogs at it in the still
Pond. And those – not you! – who hold hands by the windowsill.

II

Tired. Sleepy-eyed. Thinking about the time. I turn over and
Embrace the empty bed. It feels much the same as you
Used to. But here, in this room, at eight-thirty, the sound
Of a love-song brings me to the point: children too
Cannot get it right. This child is maybe nine
Or ten, and she listens to her record with such
Passionate understanding of the full implication
I feel almost ashamed to have forgotten so much.
Yet, my dear love, she knows nothing of the crucible,
That state of radio-active (the melting of) reason,
The union of tears with understanding, the flaring pen, the principle
Of Fuck you, Charley. Spring is the adult season
I now know. And I can't see much in it to recommend
You. Just the song, this thud, memory, and hardly a friend.

III

My head is shaking with the slow coming down of it all.
The shock and blast. The genius of deceit. The terrible
Pacts with forgiveness when I ransomed my sanity (my soul!)
Rather than lose you and it in hatred, the apple
Of revenge. I am bored with waiting for something to happen.
The woman of your body, its sense of fullness and attraction
Rings my memory of the odd, amorous vision.
But you are too far away, and I feel no sense of direction
For anything but the abstract principle of woman:
Someone who will relieve what I am told is my loneliness
And make love (never!) every night, at noon,
In the chapel, over the altar, or in genuine distress.
For what's the point of this pain in the bloody neck:
Treachery in heart and mind, treachery in sex?

IV

I meditate on Sex because of Yeats on the flight of a swallow.
Fucking hell! I am not describing that. The purpose of sex,
In my opinion, is not the received joy nor the mellow
Ecstasy. Who isn't bored with these. It's the pretext
Of life. The sum, goal, aim, target, direction,
The be-all and end-all, the common spiritual omphalos
(Which we may here compare to the belly-button):
It's the reason we go to work, wash, or buy new shoes.
It is, in fact, the thing to aim for, not a pleasure
Picked up *en route*. It is the heart of life, the heart
Of life. It would be wrong to think I'm a sexual huckster.
I am religious, and sex to me is the start
Of the pilgrimage. But what is sex? The adolescent kiss
Matured through orange-juice, brandy, L.S.D., war, marriage, or this.

V

The intensity of spring leaves nothing to be desired
But you, my dear love, holding my arm beside me.
To see you walking with that handsome joker instead
Of me, twists my optical jubilance round black infinity.
Yet the smell of jackdaws in the bushes, sweet-sweat of blossom
Against brick, the lorries that seem to purr
Because the dawn is warmer, the green, the green bloom
Of chloë on the civic copse: these are the consequences if we dare.
The discipline of forgiveness bricks my memory.
Down in the soft mud foundations rise on rock.
I will have none of the hypocrite's violence in me.
But what on earth you're going to do breaks
My patience. It's not that I do not forgive you.
It's that while you make up your mind there's nothing to do.

VI

I live under the delusion that you love me.
I am learning, however, there is no substitute
For the sexual touchstone. The kind of love you have for me
Is a load of shit. I do the work. He gets the benefit.
The joke of this shakes the sides of naked civilization
Crowding round me. The roaring of so much laughter
Sets my mind in a paranoid knot. My communication
Stops and starts with 'Ever been...?' O my daughters,
What a mother you have! Right over the horns of the moon
She threw my heart. Down, down, into the dark
She let it drop. And on to the bright Apollonian
She drove her radiant desire. And now in the squeak
And scratch of meeting him she holds the lover's inquest:
'Is this one dead, or t'other one? Which death do I like the best?'

VII

Now your loneliness. The purpose has vanished
From the new cup, the half-painted wall. The shoes
Under the dressing table belong to no one. The garden shed
Looks ugly, tatty. The children fight, chucking their toys
In childish worlds. Skin clouds the undrunk coffee.
Cigarettes rise and fall. Stale smoke hangs in the windowlight.
Friends arrive in the wrong novel. Toast turns soggy.
The dust on the carpet, for the first time, looks right.
Bills sneer contemptuously. The bottom of the wine bottle
Prefigures the corkscrew. The chapping and drying of your hands
Shakes goodbye to our first love. The morning rattle
Of the milkman stabs your snoozing heart. Holiday plans
Stink, force the head to turn. The dog farts. The door
Springs open. No one enters. There is nothing to live for.

VIII

You are more beautiful than the strong Turkish sunlight
Or dawn on the yellow sand tarmac bends by the lake.
Your arms are softer than any dawn and without a shadow of doubt
Your eyes outnumber the incidents of beauty. And I mistake
Laughter for joy – a ratbag to your good humour.
The curve of your elegant stomach surpasses the dabbling
Images, and when lost in the side contemplation of the contour
Of your bosom, I am at peace on a world of murderous squabbling.
Your hips intelligence ecstasies, and the pre-Egyptian geometry
Of your inner thigh thunders in silence, smooths the mind of its enemies.
Apples are noisy, the squirming chords of music knotty
In the ear, architecture grossly symbolic next to your sober kiss.
Your hands are my loving companions, my flowers in winter.
Your heart the erotic magnolia. Your cynicism my defender.

IX

No crackpot gambler, no cursing bus-conductor, no old
Bag vicious at the cash-till; no truth in violence,
No midnight whisper, no sunlight with another, gold on gold,
Will ever undo my laws of common sense.
To be addressed as one you cannot imagine you
Is not my lark. I know exactly what you are. Who you are,
And why. You are my tidy house, my brand new
Sheets, my fire, my roasted meat, my french liquor.
Your carpets are my undressing, your stairs my altar,
Your bathroom absolution, your bedroom evocative. You tread
The red tiles on your kitchen floor, my adult, my inventor.
Your fashion unties description, a royal glittering in the head.
Your morning tea ravishes the ghost of alcohol,
And one afternoon in your company may starry-eye this hell.

X

You are my kingdom come, my lace in red
My black-bordered blouse, my tassles, and my make-up.
You are my crystal wine, my candlelight, my head
Soft-lidded on the pillow. You are my hands of hope
Beneath the crushing blue. You are my pleasure
Circular on grass. You are my epithet, my first engender.
You are my crucible, my pestle, my mortar,
My engines, and my saws, my chisels, and my plunder.
Your eyelids reap my thought, return to murder.
And yet I am your match, your equal, and your curse.
I am your world of woe, your terror, your surrender.
You are my night of bliss, dark night of soul, and worse.
You are my bride of flesh, wedded by laws unequal
To either freedom, woman. Behold! We are terrible!

XI

Bright star, bright hope, bright light, and bright your gender.
Soft impacted lucency. Moist creole nubility.
Warmer than music. Bending with the bender
No tree in wind repeating. Smooth loose committee,
Collocating. Engineer stupendous. Interpreter unfathomless.
Ruth of reason. Spiral of desire. The burning
Flesh, famished, ravished. Flare in all distress.
Fever. Water. Water! the forehead pouring.
My love. My untouched. Skewers twisting. Hot
Shafts. God on the telephone. Cold feet. Tight
Belt. The curves of criss-delinquent, scoops of what
Burns. O! the indelible beauty! The important sight!
Colossal precision. The economy of fate. Sparks
In the eyeball. She turns, she turns. She looks.

XII

What is the colour of passion? The odour of midnight?
Only those who have not known can say.
Satiation dulls. Memory cannot get it right.
But the longing imagination sees as bright as day.
I am sick of crapological verse. I am sick of music
And all songs, whatever the beat, without the ache
And play of hearts, hearts, that thing above the stomach.
You are my niagara of blood felt where the ribs stick,
And I am not a singer. I cannot woo you
With this guitar. It's not a guitar. It's a gun and I'm
Off to kill the bad weather. The ostrich too
I'll smack with the barrel. O my love, the time
Will come when your moon will rise and mine
Will set. Then you will read my footprints in pain.

XIII

Because of my grave and serious talents I shall not spare you
One minute deceit. I am a force to be reckoned with. And if
You will not reckon with me, the glory of my art shall tear you
Limb from limb, reduce you to childhood, self-conceit, snot, and piss.
I am profoundly disturbed by your lack of respect for our
Civilization. What's it all for? The gratification of an ageing
Mum? Don't be so bloody silly. There is the hour, the hour
Of reckoning. And what do we find? We find we're waging
War, against each other. An incredibly stupid thing,
But true. In order to out-manoeuvre this absurdity
I have proposed the idea of marriage. High and lasting.
But you look upon it as just another example of me!
When you have dragged the net through the seabed of your mind
The only edible fish you will discover is this: true love is not blind.

XIV

Of the absolute barrenness of total success let me tell you.
Shit. Shit. I'm pissed off. I don't want to get drunk
By myself. Can you understand, whoever you are, it's true:
Success is in the mind? I know it's true and I drink
To all pale success, not sure of itself, in the evening
Green, by the willow, where the tennis net
Throws off a gin and tonic hallucination, a sense of being
In a more important world. And I offer yet
My warm admonition: Success, though total, is lonely,
And the arms of another encyclopedia dumb ignorance.
Therefore, like a typical bullfrog, I croak my melody,
And if one should come along, Why! the curves of chance!
My success is so complete I summon a glass of wine
To remind me the service has only just begun.

XV

What is the cause of the breakdown of any love affair?
The fact that it was meant to break down? I do not know.
It seems to me the answer may lie in the first glimpse of the other
Person. There was fire in her eyes, and, I am told,
Fire in my own. Eventually we settled down to the business
Of falling in love with each other, the eyelids incredibly
Tender, year after year. But the unpleasantness
Of fire had been overlooked. What each really wanted to be
Had been forgotten. And now it rose to claim its own
With all the ferocity of the first initial fire
We saw, with such sexual pride, in each other's turn.
I will never forget the first words I said to her
Caused her to twist on me with a kind of challenge
I fully accepted. In true love, I was thinking, you will find no revenge.

XVI

With nothing less than total abnegation
I am your contemplation. But flattery gets us nowhere.
The edge of your bikini is to me

Piraeus or Persia, the cloth of land at dawn.
And though five thousand times I have lain there
Your breast engorges my least abdominal artery.

You curl around the object of our conversation
Flesh my fever faults, my fevered fever cracks for.
And yet your brow is knitted, mother to absurdity.

Your belly like an anemone kneads my sea attraction.
You are lying in the sun your memory like a motor.
Your hips horn no pagan, rapist authority.

You are like time in a tulip, black with purple slaking
The eyes of terror: beauty, beauty in the making.

XVII

I am, in you, a tongue that has no censor.
Idolatrous all carping. And yet you pluck your eyebrows
Of course, scissor your nails, stitch the re-levelled

Hem over the jammy table. Your laughter
Is my fabulous, my rarely heard, my house
Of catalogue and glittering samples (especially the bed).

And why, while we're on it, don't I mention
Your bowl of soup, your sandwich, your guilty glare,
Cream in the wickedest interlude, joy at the windscreen,

Or, say, the hint of your stocking and shoe
Pursuing the roadside pennywort? All is fair,
I do not doubt, that praises (if it praises you):

Yet I am critical of all I might compare,
Especially (though least wrong) what you have been.

A Love Song for Saint Valentine's Day

Now every day I'll burn with light
Because dark heart you spark ablaze
Straw metaphysic's pitch-soaked night
And lightning-flash duck-thunder days.

Treading footsteps on the verge
Of highway through the seagulled sun
Towards Easthampstead Church I urge
A love forever now begun.

Trifling, ill-considered life
Around its bushy fancy beats
And booming husband bores his wife
Blasting blithering defeats.

Against the cycles of despair,
While sunny brooklet sings a bridge,
Entreaty empty pews with prayer
And Norman vaulting privilege.

The vicar's cistern hisses, drips,
The stained-glass windows flood the calm.
I put my lips upon your lips
And link you gently by the arm.

Sunlight splashes porch-worn slabs,
Seats ring antiquarian yew,
Trunks of stone fly tendered graves,
I will love you forever as I do.

The Artist's Wife

It is always the same. There is never any change in the order of things.

You wake up and the sodding bastard has done nothing about his art. The place is filthy. Above all, he has stolen your dignity.

Where you expect to find him, there is a hole. He has certainly not left a message, apart from the fact he's taken the last bottle of wine.

You look at his workroom. The windows are closed. The place is incredibly stuffy. Even you feel you'd be asphyxiated if you worked in there. You flip over his latest notebook: not a sausage. The ugly bastard has done precisely nothing for the last three months.

And all the drunken shouting I have to put up with! The unbelievable accusations! The moronic attributions of deception and counter-deception towards his own wife!

From out of the dust a torn negligée. The bone handle of a knife sticks from the strawberry jam. The sink is blocked with tea-leaves and the colander's draped with cold spaghetti. The cook book soaks up a puddle of red wine.

What's the point of carrying on with this jerk? What's the point of getting pregnant by such an oaf?

Where did I put my towel?

How can I believe in the essential goodness of such an unproductive fool? The way I look at it, I married him because I thought he was an artist, but he's turned out to be the kind of bloke who can never get down to anything. His whole life consists of nothing but an endless round of talk, drinks at the pub, and sex. The only art he understands is how to indulge himself.

I'm sick of it! The truth of the matter is, I don't believe in art any more. And I'm ashamed to admit I married a man who never did anyway.

O Woman of Christ. The Invitation.

Come not with cagey atmospheres, nor intone the accents of unacceptable obsequiousness.

Live a little longer in the unaccounted, dissemble appearance for the sake of good manners, but do not trouble yourself for light conversation.

Be proud, nor undo the attitudes of martyrs; may they co-exist in our cobbled courtyards, the tender white of certain fruit blossoms like ideas that spring to mind when happiness grows outrageous.

Be serious with fanbelts: adopt their flexibility, which is nevertheless a driving force, that our love may never be likened to the idiosyncratic dogma of camshafts.

Come with an open mind nor re-arrange your innermost secrets; may your hand-baggage be acceptable to Customs Officers, and may you smuggle through the illegal religion of your passions.

Seizmograph brainwaves; become familiar with hotness; may the afternoons in which our love expands – beyond the shuttered windows and the perspirations of actual effort – be symptomatic with fusion.

Be tender with the infirm, even as we ourselves become them; nor imagine grace in our time will last forever, even as we touch the incendiary of flesh.

Come in the morning; stay familiar till night time; but if the desire to be in the world which is not the world I know comes over you, decently state the fact and I shall not be offended.

Come with money; nor forget a walletful of time-tables; a yacht will do; and don't forget the unextinguishable.

Hear the wood-pigeon; be mournful at the right moment; but don't expect the praise of the unpraiseworthy.

Listen for the excitements of birds; deploy theology; trouble the patient flagstone with pensive effort; nor in your heart of hearts pull the green leaf from the public vineshoot.

Stay ceremonious with those in uniform; work for the increase of their personal holidays; admire the smart blouse and the immaculate shirt collar: for these are the image of the servant of the person.

Bully the waiter; force him to concede the divinity of his person; bash him with facts, like the greater part of what we come to drink.

Terrify the nutshell; make the few remaining hairs in its curious and empty hammock swing your soul to sweet oblivion; nor toss it on the unswept pavement.

Collect innuendoes, that our minds may be at peace; but if you should come down roads of warlike light, do not expect me to be less than courageous.

Batter the door of the eyeball with the white and just walking-stick of the spiritual blind, then give them back their stick, and come to my side with figs and newspapers.

Split the implausible with coincidence; make life a little more interesting; take off your clothes; and be the habits of ten thousand people, soothing the invisible with their generous humanity.

Lance the inaccurate; cause the appreciation of murder a lower notch on the stock exchange.

Interest mammals in humility; teach them radiance; do not be hungry to stroke the kitten, nor waste a lot of time with sleepy dogs: let them go their own ways splendid in workless inheritance.

Drink with soldiers, that knowledge may be more free-flowing; nor grow paranoic with military officers, whose wives have given birth to erroneous mythologies.

Try to be nice to yourself, though many wouldn't; be reasonable with personal differences; and don't expect a lot from an all time love.

Keep your eye on your origin, who come from the mountains of my desire, and never as you sweat, the uncertainty in your face, think I am indifferent, who can feel nothing greater than the praise of your person.

The Corpus Christi of Womanhood

Assault without warning   burn the registers of memory.

Roll over beneath the sheet   let me see your body
   who watch your mind   unrolling behind your sleep.

What trust in all things   a shape to drive men mad
   sprawled on your back   your almost orange tan
   at peace with the tangled sheets.

The life I had   Where is it?   Gone.   The faith I had
   Where is it?   Gone.

The temptations of the flesh are glowing in your abdomen.

Your bones melt to water as your touch is pure.

Beautiful woman   reliable as fire   lie there awhile
   let me look   let me wonder   sleeping in my life
   open to the womb   and to and through   all beyond.

See me to reason   guide me from your navel
   to the prayerbook   and back again.

May I pray that God   who alone can take responsibility
   for making you   will touch your flesh
   with the glow of sanctity   the Corpus Christi
   of Womanhood   soothing   soothing.

Before the Time of the Sundial

1

What raptures in a woman's body, see, she breathes
Oceans of containment, sucking my index finger,
The intelligence of the world her eyes, the rest the waves
Of scampering knowledge seeking to understand her.

Liquid with authority, the lazy miracles roll
In beads of sweat and tears down her enormous smile,
While I, shaking from the shock of knowing so much, hold
Eternal form before the time of the sundial.

She blinks so slowly, I could compose a book
Before an eyelash returns to where it started.
She touches with such eloquence, believe me, were I blind,

I could read the scripture of her naked look.
No man may feel her fingers and hope to find
In the paradise of woman mankind brokenhearted.

2

Enough. Enough. The surging powers renew
The spring floodtides of man, the sap of feeling.
Rush to be born, dear twin, turn under blue
Brand new skies to see me likewise reeling.

Shall dance be more? Shall wise men sigh no louder?
Shall trees emblaze in praise if we're not holding
Each other in our arms, no lovers prouder?
Shall life unfold with no such love unfolding?

What theme is this? Truelove? The kind an angel
Spreads by rumour behind a golden hand?
As when Saint Francis said, "I'll get a daughter."?

And so I praise my days our locked limbs mangle
Down to the pith of love, our pestle and our mortar
Grinding us to glory like sea the unprinted sand.

3

She's with me now and slow my blood unreasons
My latitude and longitude of thought,
For she unseats my judgement, crowns me her seasons'
Emperor of morals and what cannot be bought.

As day expires, she gentles me with legs
Crossed in jetty nylons blazing to be embraced,
As, looping satin breasts, her necklace begs
No question of her suit or woman's taste.

My God, dear fellow, you see her sitting there
(Here, have a gin, the bar looks wild tonight)
Well, she's my red-belted lady, belting bare

My mind-whipped body, man, for she is rich
Bullion unbarred, our workdays burnished bright
Since gold knew gold and neither which is which.

4

We scent the sweetness tender as the trees'
Brave young leaves breathing an infinite wind.
For this is courage, the trust in all that frees
Purpose in life from the all-embittering mind.

Tendrils of praise, our fingers cradle buds,
Our darlings of the moment, as in our arms
We taste the spring we are through parted lips
Feasting on flesh the common sunshine warms.

We stop and sit and sip white wine and talk.
There's much too much to say, yet speech is heard
Praising the day we learnt one simple word

Culled from oblivion redeems. We name with ease
The blossoms we would die for, the erupting trees,
As arm in arm together we resume our walk.

5

Joy of my days, delight of my nights, hard partner
Walking the long paving-stones of Chelsea Embankment,
The sparkling light dandles on the grey river
The first principle of our love's bedazzlement.

You are no lady pricing the golden air,
Nor priceless statue turning in a glass museum,
For we've become one light, this light we share
Dancing the global stone through hand-held heaven.

Conspiracy of spring, behold in her
The green and lush amazement of yourself,
For you are what she is, this bed unfolding

Out of the black catastrophe of nightmare.
Redressed in clothes she hands me, I am the wealth
The rich aspire to in their tallest building.

6

That day in Marlow. Now I'm driven wild,
My brain awake with images of love.
Behold my sun, around it tumbling gold
Boiling into blue the young leaves crave.

Behold my Thames (crowned with a dozen chicks
Skedaddling the molten gold) flow into time
Serener than petals wedding the churchbright ducks,
The spritely gardener rolling the antique lawn.

Behold my horses snorting the hoof-kicked sky,
My Elizabethan manor house, my skiff
Slicing the silence aeons puff to blossoms

Of such perfection wings thrash past my eye
Swooping on water now two immortal swans
Glide by the copse where you and I make love.

7

Jesus Christ it's horrible this pain
Invisible to doctors or the good,
For I am on the rack of what I am
Stung by the redhot pokers of her blood.

Though God I love, though sex I praise, though life
Is troubled not at all by what it kills,
I'll take this ghastly torture in my stride
And teach myself what loving woman means.

This dreadful wine, this cigarette on fire
With smoke I suck to stem my fever's flow,
Cannot control the madness I adore,

The loving of her supernatural soul.
She beats my broken brains, my body's all,
As, stung by love, I taste the love I know.

8

Serene, o moon, you torture me with lies.
While I got drunk, you lit my darkened lawn
With nets of light, and set her there, to gaze
In rapture at you captured in my garden.

Why don't you gloat less brightly? Set T.V.
Full in the forehead of your jealous mind?
Sit her on my sofa drinking wine with me
While I admire her in my drunken kind?

No mercy, moon, I see, you choose to shine
Making a monkey of my rival face:
She is so free french windows cannot hold her

As on her face, as on her fragrant shoulder,
You drop your balm, your soul-enchanting lies,
And steal from me what heaven knows is mine.

9

Behold the dark, alone, with nothing in it,
Except despair, your poverty, and death.
Then, like a switch within, electric light
Broadcast through the bedroom where you breathe.

This is my state. I'm richer than the wild
And idle rich burning the bloom of youth,
For love alone is money, and the gold
The rich transcend the struggle to this truth.

Quicker than blinkers, love decides the price
Of oxygen and hydrogen no less
By which we breathe and eat and come to grace

Glowing in the knowledge of each other.
Ah yes, it's true, the love without the lover
Is like the bowl without the grains of rice.

VI

Narratives

A Citizen in a Monastery in a Time of War

Two miles above the sea in a silent monastery
Unpaced by monk or visitor, I sit at a long concrete refectory table
And look out on tranquillity. Above me, spreading over the inhabitation,
Is a giant plane tree, big enough to cool a village square.
The blue sea stretches away and the green hills sweep upwards,
The sun beats down and the birds sing in the incense-scented pine trees.
The cells of the monks are still and the shadowed courtyard
Dappled with a cool warmth, the warmth of June.
Around me roars the war, both upwards and downwards,
And on all sides, the bloody logic irrefutable,
The law of cause and effect furious and bloody.
There is no end, human on human, like trains shooting into tunnels
They pursue the inevitable doom. Sorrow. Sorrow. O holy God,
To you, who made the atom, inlaid the principles of ladders and water-
    melons,
Who comprehends insanity, swims in the blood of the unborn,
Who touches conception, increases without constriction,
Who has no trouble with mathematics, nor can misunderstand astro-
    physics,
Who implicitly rejected emptiness yet made it your very own doorstep;
To you, who focus sharply on everything, like the glassed eye of a
    jeweller,
Unbamboozled by perspective, unconcerned about motion
Nor the terrible traffic in explosions dotting the infinite;
To you, like the finger of a peasant woman pushing a thimble
Driving the inscrutable steel that patches up division,
Who loves the infant instinct to prayer and the awkwardness of adults
Congregating in their crash-helmets of self-consciousness;
To you, the glory of the world, at last I come
To ravish my own self with the paradox you inhabit
And I must transcribe, foreordained by Permission.
You are my mighty dictator and I am here unworthily
Scratching dictation, a blue pen on a white page,
Unhurried to begin, nor impatient to continue, your ever-loving
    secretary,
Summoned from drunkenness and the inscooping orbits of pretty
    women,
Dazzled by opportunity, crushed by the gravity of it all,
But functioning, apprehensive, ready.

I sing the Unsplit God, the father adamantine,
The furious bastard, the lethal witch, the administrator,
The stinking origin, the foul-mouthed, yellow-belly poisoning.
I sing the trap-door cunning, the round-the-corner back-up;
The double-cross, the deceit; the lazer whip and the horses
Molten gold them all, flowing in the rivers of precession.
I praise how the marble of mountains and the cotton wool of doctors
Coexist in the world of the kneecap of the Almighty.
I praise the vigil, the career, and the compassion
Peopled in conference in the lip of the Aforesaid.
I praise the jail, the injustice, and the juror
Battling it out in the elbow the Unsplit God is scratching.
I praise the rain, the lightning flash, and the thunder
An incident in his fingernail he taps for amusement.

See here the story of first beginnings,
A concrete bench and a morning-glory flower
Co-exact, even as the mournful purple of bougainvillaea
Heaves into radiance. See here now
The monastery is to the pill-box what tranquillity is to the machine-gun.
Both have their purpose, you say. But I say, Not so.
The pill-box and the machine-gun have their purpose,
But the monastery and the tranquillity are at the end of purpose.
For this is the edge of the world, the plane tree fluttering.
For this is the vigil of mankind, the senior hiding-place,
The refuge of the scholar, the saint and the scoundrel.

A copper bell hangs in the branches of a tree.
An empty chair in the courtyard faces the sea where waves
Like sub-atomic particles in a cloud-separation chamber
Sink to oblivion, and the edge of the sea is tinted aquamarine.
The monastery is deserted (brandy bottles strewn below the foundations)
Except for the closed doors of five monks at prayer. On a neighbouring hill
The radar of the army turns swiftly in the heat.
Soldiers dine. A fishing vessel hugs the coastline. I hear
The cry of the tortured, those instantly maimed, and the dead,
The lacerated, the burned, the dying, and the unloved.
The songs of the freed, the miraculous recoverer, the enchanted parent,

The lucky, the friends in wild bars, the loving and the trustful
Help soothe imagination, but What is going on? is the only real question.

   The wind shakes early fruit from a tree. The sun casts no shadow.
A private yacht assaults the entire blue of the sea.
Courting birds flash between treetops. Even the rubbish sparkles
And a wild goat with gold eyes and a shaggy coat
Enters the dappled courtyard. The trunk of the tree, hollow,
And big enough to house a children's party,
Grows out of the ground with the massive conviction of an elephant's
    foot.
The bony elbows of the giant boughs uphold a starry dome of leaves
Intertinted with the palest of blues sparkling at the zenith.
A hemisphere of water in a glass shivers on the concrete table top
And loose crumbs of bread blow hither and thither in the uncertain
    wind.

   Here in a cell where the air is dark and quiet
Light flows through with the glowing information of the sun.
The uneven whitewashed walls stand two feet thick.
The cell is furnished by silence.
Outside, the local insect population
Seethes on its urgent mission, and the hooves of goats
Can be heard running along a wall. Truth is how
One man's life finds peace in such a place
Looking out on the sea beneath the shadow of the fruit trees
Footed and shouldered by hills, visited by birds,
Drinking from a well of clear water in the uncut rock,
Stable in body and mind, praying with others
Morning, noon, and evening beneath the all-inspiring plane tree.
Nothing can collapse in the atmosphere of prayer.
Murder cannot move the peace which comes with love.

O Mother Heal Your Son

I fell asleep and dreamed a dream.
The world lay like a globe in night;
The sun shone like a golden beam.
The stars and planets too were bright.
Great galaxies like specks behind
Majestic space sublimely spun.
I searched the infinite of mind.
 O mother heal your son.

I went where water laps the rock
And quiet pools greet storm-tossed fish.
I saw the Pleiades unlock
And diamonds spilling in a dish.
But heard the radar of the past
Booming like a hunter's gun:
The miracles of hope don't last.
 O mother heal your son.

Through dusty vaults of books by floors;
By cherrybloom on new-mown grass;
Through flaps of mosques, cathedral doors;
And bridges summer students pass:
I searched the places where I'd known
Inspired, the air of vision stun.
Your death had turned them all to stone.
 O mother heal your son.

The morning sky no brighter blue
Shocks on my inward brooding gaze.
The trees of early summer too
No greener in their fountains blaze.
The loves I have, dissolving night,
Persuade me like undoubting sun.
They prove, though wrong, their love is right.
 O mother heal your son.

At night I watch the moon float by;
The curtains rustle in the breeze;
A cat is walking in the sky,
And nothing in myself agrees.
I rise and dress and make some tea
And drink it as the flashbacks run.
Your love was always home to me.
    O mother heal your son.

I take a book and find a page.
I cannot read the lucid text.
It is your battlefield with age,
Fresh corpses, where my own is next.
It breaks my heart to see you die
So nobly, every battle won
Now all are lost, for there you lie.
    O mother heal your son.

The heaps of flowers rot on your grave.
The seasons change. My child appears.
The antique ecstasy of love
Drives the dynamo of years.
Time generates new life again.
The spark of sex: it's all begun.
No greater love knows greater pain.
    O mother heal your son.

Sheep and lambs graze by the church.
Rooks are raucous in the elms.
In blue, a dazzling silver birch
The cornfield overwhelms.
I note the instinct to admire
Stoops with grief but soars to fun
Through which we parachute to fire.
    O mother heal your son.

My shed by day looks calm but dark.
A sunbeam slants across the wall.
I take a chisel from the rack
And chip a mortise for a table.
The mallet's long then silent knock
Sounds in the houses labour done,
Nor that I'm hollowed out by shock.
   O mother heal your son.

The shocks of life come down like blows
Crushing the spirit in us set.
Will helpless attitudes expose
Or find us more triumphant yet?
How may we bear, who feel such grief
Squarely in our hearts, that none,
While others suffer, find relief?
   O mother heal your son.

Do not be sad, when this is just.
Justice is the least of me.
My love is more than dust to dust,
And freedom not so free.
But grief like a journey takes us far
Beyond the place where it begun:
My brother's lone exploding star.
   O mother heal your son.

Bit by bit he breaks apart.
The speed of light slow motion knows.
The more glorious his heart
The more its quick explosion slows.
Our blood like meteors displayed,
As God is truly three-in-one,
My sister and two brothers prayed:
   O mother heal your son.

I prayed that others might explore
My lens of life to see their own
Virulent motives huge as war
Submicroscopic in the bone.
I prayed once more, because I see
Holier than thou, my pride has won
My microbe heart to irony.
   O mother heal your son.

Long in the mountains in retreat
With half a life but all my heart,
I heard the sticks of passion beat
My conscience in a cage apart.
Then took a saw and cut some planks,
The sawdust winnowing in the sun,
And built a house in praise and thanks.
   O mother heal your son.

Long in the mountains in retreat
I lived this life with all my heart
And touched true peace but found defeat
Taught me the penitence of art.
Drunk in the evenings, there I'd sit
Hallowed (bright fire) by what you'd done.
But no, I could never get used to it.
   O mother heal your son.

Back in the city I made my way
Jumbled in tunnels; a million lives
Coming and going; commutable day
The sum of the sacred and secular drives.
Nothing cohered. I felt my mind
Shattered by impact. What had I done?
Life in retreat was making me blind.
   O mother heal your son.

The tender traffic of the dawn
Light like love's first certain touch
That instant when a child is born
And praise itself seems nothing much:
Two turtle-doves alone have sung
Such bliss in life, till panics stun.
The flustered parents eat their young.
  O mother heal your son.

What ghostly hand my stifled scream
Reached out to soothe through that long night?
It was your own. And then my dream
Broke like an ocean on my sight.
I lay awake and watched the way
The holy family moves as one.
Nor was there anyone to say
  O mother heal your son.

Lines for My Unborn Son

PART 1

Prelude

I lay alone. The moon lay on the sea
Chilly as steel and grey as polished lead.
Like hope, it shone, warm with what's to be
Skittling the waves (and graves of millions dead).
Reflected sun, I felt it on my face
Kissing the beach and each spun star the night
Saucered and flung the Milky Way of space.
   What father loved who brought you to this sight?

I lay alone. Transfixed by trees, the sky
Blazed with ideas: the bear that stalks the pole,
The southern cross, the zodiac, the eye
With which the bull surveys the virgin whole.
The night was fair. A thousand-petalled rose
Drank in my garden the perfume of her peers.
Long water drips. Long tired eyelids close.
   What father loved who brought you to these tears?

I lay alone. Your bed was cradled white.
Your sheets embroidered blue along the edge.
Your mother's head had dimmed the natural light
Of candleflame candescent on the ledge.
Your father leaned, and, two, we told how green
Paradise arose; and huddled humankind,
Hutted by fires, kindled all that's been.
   What father loved now this unwisely blind?

"Is this a bridge? What's safe?" I heard a voice
Challenge the tundra of the mythic mind.
We lay alone, the parents of the choice
To love or die, yet find the two combined.
We sensed you there, our double-bed ablaze
In paisley flames our tender sleep enjoyed,
Now you are born, who crossed the bridge of praise.
   What father loved who brought you love destroyed?

Hampstead

Seagulls swoop the Heath. The concave blue
Curls into clouds that drench the distant rooves.
Leaves fly the trees, and old is what was new
Ripped from the force round which the sacred moves.
Look, the millions dead, their quaint, old-fashioned dress
(The sunlight glinting on the monk-smoothed stone)
Downed in the flashlit cities suns caress.
    What father brought you to a nuclear zone?

And then at tea, my worldly winter gaze
Etched by the hackwork of a maddened heart,
Soothing myself, because I've learnt the ways
The antidote philosophy practises this art.
Then hate me well, because that fatal word,
'Philosophy', cuts men to the quick:
So many dead whose deaths life makes absurd?
    What father loved who makes a dead man sick?

I watch the buses thread the city streets,
And shops unlock, and meditate the day.
I was the drunk whose suicide completes
The gutter where there's nothing left to say.
"There is nowhere to go. There's never been a place
Where love redeems or dares forgive the cost.
Is Adolf Hitler sanctified by grace?"
    What father loved who brought you to the lost?

School and Oxford

I grew and learned. I studied. All my school
Were rapt attention to a white-hot truth.
We watched the elders' words induce the rule
And infant minds to crude, rebellious youth.
Alone I trembled, standing on the ring
That circles fact from fiction, till it warps.
Each life's a glass that's rubbed enough to sing.
    What father's love foresaw each shattered corpse?

From school I passed to university.
Most loved the place. I tilled the fields of mind
Till harvest came. Then set myself to see
The truth and prove the logic of the find.
Research at last, I blew the dust from shelves
Collating knowledge uncombined before,
Till (breathless) I unearthed our buried selves.
   What father loved who brought you to this war?

Psychotic drugs' and drink's ten thousand eyes
Taunting, "You're finished", paraded in my head.
And it was true. Yet still I felt surprise:
"You've been elected to the living dead".
I stopped to check. My touch was out of joint.
And love remembered laughed my life to scorn:
Around, vile space; within, a vanished point.
   What father loved who brought you to be born?

PART 2

Life

I set to work, though jobs were hard to get.
So, self-employed, I stripped the paint from pine
In tanks of caustic soda, scrubbing wet
Wardrobes, doors, and dressers till they'd shine.
'Antiques' I called them, roping to a car
The auctioned relics of outgoing lives.
Small wonder no one mourned my burnt-out star.
   What father blooms when unemployment thrives?

In ten long years, some jobless, I advanced
To selling books (from scrubbing on my knees).
With such inheritance as ours,
I hadn't thought that luxury would please.
But strove at harder beauty, which I found
Derelict and drunken and in debt,
Proud of itself because it stood its ground.
   What father loved not this fraternal yet?

Greece

I went to Greece, my cornerstone in time,
Democratized and sanctified in Christ.
The scars of war were healing, but the lime-
White houses seldom underpriced.
I bought a ruin; rebuilt it; with my wife
I settled down when spring was in the air.
At last I saw the sunny side of life.
    What father's love left nothing for his heir?

By day I laboured in the cypress trees
And chopped them clean and peeled away the bark,
Then dragged them on my hip to act as beams;
And drank at evenings in the candled dark.
I patched a door and windows on the sun
Sailing in blue profounder than the sky.
Electrified and fired, the plumbing done,
    What father loved who loved no more than I?

I give you Pedro, smoking, as he hauls
Hods of cement to his shoulder where it bleeds,
And Agathon Liatsos on the walls
Reinforcing concrete to my needs.
And tiling on the roof, I hand you one
Perched at work, the mountain's steep degrees
Without a scaffold, trowelling alone.
    What father loved more noble men than these?

I give you Leonidas as he trowells;
And staggering Theodoras, his arms
Filled with a rock he daintily unspills,
And Stathis blowing bamboo from his palms.
There's Taki, too, chipping shape to stone
(Though more accustomed to his café store)
And young Elias hammering alone.
    What neighbours loved who loved your father more?

Asimakopoulos the proud
Kosta the carpenter walks by.
He made the floor and casements and he showed
Me how to think (a fledgling how to fly).
Last, Agathon Liatsos once again.
No nobler man has ever crossed my path.
He wears a golden cross. He's president. And sane.
　I would be proud worth half his epitaph.

London

Oh London caught me in a vicious mood.
Half mad, I chafed on poverty's long chain.
In all I'd done, no money had accrued,
And drunk to the world, I howled my pain.
My mother dead, most friends dead too, or mad,
I found salvation in the art of verse,
Which taught my pain rejoicing in the sad.
　What father loved who died of Adam's curse?

Still as the dew that hangs above a lake
On thorny bushes before that tree was cursed,
I hold my head immobile as I take
In the meaning energy must burst:
We love and work, because we see the prize
Rich wisdom steals the show for, in our name:
Money is trust, and trust is money's eyes.
　What father loved who never felt the same?

So labour now has found its true dominion,
And what I earn I relish as I pay
For debts and beauty and the odd companion
Half-hidden in a bar or common day.
I execute my life to make a poem,
And kiss as you (the next generation curled)
Will do yourself, because you know whom
　Your father loved who brought you to the world.

VII

The Impenetrability of Silence

A Nuclear Epiphany

Poetry is the medium of the complex quality of the blest.

It does not seek to define but to reveal.

It seeks to show us that we all have an emotional relationship with each other, and not just with each other but with every speck of dust.

It seeks to show us that though we may not love the ant, nor may we love our neighbour; or might willingly and proudly bomb and mutilate our brother.

It seeks, in other words, to reveal ourselves to each other before ourselves destroy each other.

It seeks, most of all, to illuminate intelligence with passion, and passion with the light of the eye, the music of the ear, and the touch of the lover.

It remains sure-footed, stuck-to-the-ground, because it has a poise and a sense of balance mastered through experience.

It can twirl with a mannequin or prance on a catwalk, but it will never sulk like a model nor grow restive with foreign observers.

It looks at the moon like a catpaw toys absentmindedly, imagination untrammelled in a New Jerusalem of chatting stars.

Bank balancers lean from their ledgers, students of English look up from their desk-tops, Formula One racing drivers glance over their shoulders, and milk-maids drop buckets – for it is passing by.

It has the quality of paperclips in bulb light, chromium in neon, or bread in daylight.

It walks with an apple chewed at the mouth by a newborn youth in her first pair of jeans.

It reckons by minutes on its fingers as its eyes draw in the skyline of centuries.

It preaches its own modernity to disguise its antique penumbra, and scribbling scholars, each one at two hundred words a minute, shall sit throughout eternity and describe no more than a particle.

A born-again preacher shall feel it stun him, even as a tennis ball slaps the back of his neck.

Trivial liars shall feel its icy fingers on the pubis, even as it hallows their wretchedness in a dawn of dissolving envy.

Mushrooms shall sprout in its honour, every one a normal species, and ten thousand hands the world over shall pluck and sniff its unforgettable aroma.

Night-time in Rio and castanets shall announce it, even as bells in cathedrals resound throughout a priesthood.

Democratic millionaires fan their faces with its many leaves, and ponder the application of its flick-book fertility.

Musicians pluck it from the shivering string, and politicians in Whitehall shall trip up on it an agreeable moment one lunch-hour.

The glorious haughty giraffe blinks in its honour, and cheetahs leaping the plain shall grow forgetful of antelopes.

Typesetters shall peer from their keys, eager as eyes that race out of water, to track its path through the office.

And lizards that lick the skies shall for a moment ponder the Great Comedienne.

The whirling dervish shall think of his mother, and ten dynasties of Chinese peasants shall coalesce in a shining fingernail.

The morning in Egypt shall begin with the evening prayers in San Francisco, and the crying of infants in Adelaide shall antedate the officiations of the Prelate of All England.

Dogs shall drop off the wings of aeroplanes, and wake up in parachutes, and scheming men-of-letters shall fall asleep in the Sunday newspapers and wake up in the *chordae tendonae*.

The duplication of expertise shall become a thing of no interest, and all shall walk in the valley of dreams a little less afraid and a little more dead.

No understanding of life shall be preceded by less than a death, and all the cherries in the imagination of spring shall hurtle the saint to no erroneous conclusion.

Butter shall melt in the freezer, and straight lines shall accommodate the profile.

Bees shall enter the two-dimensional, as honey drips in the love-making of criminals.

Medical men will invoke Saint Augustine, and Saint Augustine will queue with the hopeless at the door leading back to existence.

Angels will preen their wings on the brasswork of laidback motorcyclists, and 40,000 revs a minute will fail to register in the fine tuning of holy communion.

The log books of sea captains will contain traces of the sanctity of the sea, and raincoated West End dancers will shout for joy in their mirror-bulbed dressing-rooms.

Teeth shall tinkle in the stainless steel dishes of dentists, and the fingernail clippings of Princesses will find their ways down the back seats of Bentleys.

Gardeners shall comb their heads with mud-caked fingers, and the evening skies in Bromley South will come to resemble the innermost glories of the sunshattered raindrop.

Pigeons shall swoop without reason, and sparrows will spit bullets of dignity.

Ladies will step into bed with gentlemen, and the living man shall love the living woman, even into the incredible of the first creation.

Churches shall walk, and the slave brick sing.

Children shall see the instruction of all adulthood, and the brave wave shall cease to exist, as the tidal wave, O Poseidon, slips through the reason of the existence for anything.

Nuns shall somersault on razorblades, and the literary critic shall deduce the infallible formula.

The ancient alchemist shall materialize as the fertilized ovum, and the tender traffic in eyelashes shall usher the loved one down miraculous avenues of flesh.

Indescribable torture shall taunt the impregnable ego, and rivers of rotting flesh shall dwarf the almighty Amazon.

Blood will glow like wind in velvet curtains, and the indecipherable shall stalk the articulate statesman.

Rumours shall rebound from lonely concrete, and the information of engineered genes shall prove inadequate for the reparation of instinct.

Doctors shall feel their pulses, and lack understanding of hitherto inhuman music, and lesbians shall prowl at large advertising monosexual comic-books.

Homosexual males shall climb up telegraph poles, to get a better view, but the unfamiliar sun shall shine on all like a dithyrambic migraine.

The senses shall change places with each other, but it won't help, and the dissolution of fleshly integrity shall presage the nightmare of lambs.

Men shall die for a wink, and women shall give birth to exclamation marks.

Time shall laugh, and the mechanisms of science preach the folly of ingenuity.

Space will warp like a sheet of tin, and the worp-worp of shaken tin shall lunify an elegant movie actor.

Cheesegraters will cohere with diamond tiaras, and obsolescent fishing tackle will hook the snorting leviathan.

Tumblers shall fill with aqueous intensity, and the critic of the poet will taste the incendiary of air.

Ten thousand inches will be crammed into the metrical foot, and the boots of the American Army shall pound in the mind of the unjust person.

Justice herself shall sing, and the mountain waterfall shall respond, even as the ovens roar, and humanity enters and leaves a neverending furnace in a pitiless paradox of understanding.

Goats shall comb their beards, and the centipede shall strum an implacable guitar of legs.

Men of evil will bow to the first steps of innocence, even as innocent genius itself dreams up the unconsciousness of torture.

Lives shall be over before they've begun, and the attitudes of the invincible shall know the full decrepitude of ignorance.

Bombs will mew in the disappearance into origin, and the inconceivable agony at the heart of us all will make itself felt in every organism that ever was.

God shall appear, and every creature shall divine; none shall miss the point; and God will shiver in the realization of his total impracticality.

Ministering angels shall restore him to his infinitude, and the fantastic mystery at the heart of human intention shall once again fail to notice him slip by as he dons the impenetrability of silence.

II

Wines will serve their purpose, and the engineering of hangovers shall take up the mood of contrition.

Tongues will be spread on biscuits, and the psychosomatic will twinge an intelligence of inhumanity.

The chimes of doorbells will anticipate Armageddon, and the ash flipped in ash-trays will preach a revolution in gentleness.

Secretaries in insurance companies will lock themselves in the loo, and male porters in prominent auction houses will swallow bottles of aspirin in futile attempts at suicide.

Guns will melt, and the toasting-fork will herald the politics of humbug; and nothing that ever was will knock on the front doors of wideawake commuters, even as the morning glory flowers and the paving stones in Holborn High Street flake off from the earth and shower at re-entry into gravity.

Popsingers will say, "Oh God", and surgeons will resign their implements.

Miners' suppers will hiss on abandoned stoves, and the ladylike charlady will drop to her knees and pray in earnest to the God of the duster.

The successful will feel the pull of their unacknowledged commonalty, and the self-righteous prostitute will waver between fifty pound notes and a drawerfull of frilly knickers.

The television, like the houseplant, will broadcast a wider story, and the china ducks on the wall will fly across the infinite.

Postcards will curl, and the unannounced visit from relatives will be delayed till The New Year; and the unwelcome tax-inspector will be recognized as the sole hope in a world utterly abandoned.

No-hope alcoholics will lift an unaccustomed eyebrow, and the wood-shavings of industrial carpenters will orchestrate a ballet of unbecoming.

Seas will apologize for insolent behaviour, and the insurgent mountain will practise a choirboy's humility.

Latitude will fry like longitude, and the ship alone on the Indian Ocean shall feel an unwelcome intimacy.

Incontravertible facts will bow to superior reason, and superior reason herself shall dance to the whips of alacrity.

Nine men holding death warrants shall feel what it means to be hunted, and rum-sipping actresses in Barbados shall approach the ocean with devout intentions.

Rhythms hitherto unheard shall ricochet round squash courts in Mayfair, and lazy miracles shall get up like lionesses and waddle from the shadows of fire-fringed oak trees.

Human intelligence shall seem a thing of the past, and able-bodied computers shall look thoroughly silly in a world peopled by nightmares.

Human communication will proceed as usual at a speed faster than light, but speeds far in excess of either shall tap both on the shoulder and wink and blink and arrest them.

Nothing will be easy to come by, and never-ending nausea shall have a field day; the spanner in the works will glow like lightning, and the sons and daughters of men and women will realise the insurgency of Blue Ice.

Bones will cling like leaves to the wire in the unfooling wind, and lives will be blown from their spines like waves from the sea in the uncautious hurricane.

None of this shall be deemed rhetorical, and the expanded pupil in the Cheshire Cat shall at last dilate to its full implication.

Life will pass us by, and we shall wonder, Whatever was it that made us disbelieve in death, like death itself a thing of the past, as we float in the impenetrability of silence.

III

Freed at last from conventional constrictions, sun-loving mountebanks shall realise just how anarchic Our Mountebank really is.

Newts shall spin on their tails, and four million screws in the pigeon-holes of iron-mongers shall pirouette in a maddening fandango.

Zebra crossings shall peel off like sunburn, and the advertisements for mineral water shall be slapped around the fuselages of disintegrating B-52s.

Electrons shall beg for mercy, and the haunted quark of the physicist shall plod the streets in billboards.

Nothing as simple as the wiring of the City of London shall scintillate the all-understanding imagination, as the implication of whatever is, like Gothic music, booms through the crevices of whatever is in the way.

Geese shall ignite, and the magazines in stationers shall vanish like snowflakes on Canadian lakes.

Love shall disconnect, and money shall wave goodbye.

Loneliness shall embrace the individual, and the individual shall become the impenetrability of silence.

IV

The lone visionary eye shall be visited by the unredeemable devil, and the hopscotch idiot shall proclaim the Lord's Prayer imprecise.

The bus queues in Cowley Oxford shall be blown away like autumn, and the tender heiffer in rural England shall disappear in a radiant summer of plutonium.

Big media chicks shall marinate, and the wedding rings of famous impressarios shall twirl like the saucers of drunken psychiatrists.

Morning shall blacken, and the midnights of cocaine sniffing treasurers shall flare up like the incandescence of Auschwitz.

Seriousness shall be deemed frivolous, and the frivolous shall inherit a golden twinkling.

Mothers shall clap burnt cylinders to breasts which have long since ceased to exist, and the waking dreamer shall roll over in bed where none of this ever happened.

Forgiveness shall germinate in a world empty of human beings, and the tappeted thunder of an internal combustion engine shall be like piano keys on the impenetrability of silence.

V

The inadequate forethought of lovers shall imply a colosseum of dying relatives, and the aftermath of ten thousand million orgasms shall create a world where one small thought gives peace.

Numbers shall add up to zero, and the counting houses of my lords the Rothschilds shall radiate the intensity of metallic gold on fire.

Neutered cats will run for ineffective cover, and the crews of Chinese laundromats will witness the priceless oracle.

Paint will bubble before it has dried, and the tiny blood vessels examined through opthalmoscopes by eye surgeons shall look back with an unmistakable and terrifying implication.

Politics shall animate nature, and everywhere the news will arrive not through the letterbox but the more succinct convenience of everywhere.

Religion shall seem no different from total warfare, and total warfare itself shall immediately become outdated.

Matter shall irradiate the majesty of God, and life will sizzle at last as prayer emblazons the disappearing mind.

Thermos flasks shall roll like tumbleweed, and the heroin addict shall become immortalised as the atoms of the needle shake hands with the atoms of the flesh.

Junior doctors in hospital mortuaries shall sense an uninvited ecstasy, and small infants crawling across carpets shall resound like musical instruments to the harmonies of Physical Science.

Stereo music shall take on unfamiliar dimensions, and the teeth on a carpenter's saw shall be like a zip on the impenetrability of silence.

VI

Poems shall nevermore exist, and prayer shall be housed in museums.

Saintly people will snap like twigs, and the future of personality will be all in the past.

Time will have ticked its bit, and the shape of space will have finally folded its volume.

Gravity will give up its demands, and the laws of aerodynamics will kneel immobile in stone.

Tortured aristocrats will cease to howl, and the nightingale shall twinkle forever in the ear and the eye of the torturer.

The printing-press will print wine, and the wine-press shall shoot forth a dry alphabet.

Sunsets shall be eradicated, and the miraculous emptiness of space shall throw off its last vestment of illusion.

The medium of all media will burn between galaxies, and the speeding spaceship shall seem like a paperboat on the Atlantic.

Tunnelling pot-holers shall emerge into daylight even as they touch pointblank rockface, and the librarian in the city vault shall enter the impenetrability of silence.

VII

Because of the sounds of children laughing and the roar of automobiles on the Hammersmith flyover, the leopards in London Zoo and the bus conductors in Greater Manchester shall open the chords of a nuclear epiphany.

Because of the inflationary quality of yeast and the unwanted beercans in Hyde Park Corner, a gambler's mistress in a pale blue Ford Mustang shall put on the mantle of transcendental illumination.

Because of the laws of solid geometry and the bloodymindedness of terminal incontinence, a bishop's mitre and the scrotum of an undiscovered murderer will melt into unity, even in the eyeball of a theosophic letter writer.

Because of the translucency of the beerglass and the insurmountability of the weather on Mount Everest, a baby will be born into the swaddling bands of an almighty angel and twenty-five taxi-drivers in a traffic-jam by Harrods shall feel the touch of the impenetrability of silence.

VIII

And then because of the poor manners of distant relations and the boring incumbency of an incipient cocktail circuit, ducks will fly south from Peking and the coffee cups in the Bar Italia in Soho will illuminate the crocodiles setting out to river in the bloodstream of an unprotected shopkeeper.

And then because of books in cardboard boxes and the unpurchased chocolate biscuits in village Post Offices, glaziers will extract splinters of glass from the flesh of an infinite present while the steam irons of semi-naked girls in Chelsea bedsitters smooth the wrinkles on the face of The Great Eavesdropper.

And since there are fish in aquaria and the great wave has yet to touch the shingle on the beaches at Sheringham, murderers impregnate civilians and a conflagration of burnt toast smokes in the eyes of a curate's daughter.

And then because small holes are bored in public lavatories and the syphilitic spirochete glorifies in its own sexual intercourse, ten million brain cells immolate in every idea and the intuitions of meditating soccer players assume the dimensions of Chartres Cathedral.

And since because of hymn books and the never-ending tread of shoes, lights are switched off in bedrooms and limbs engage the impenetrability of silence.

IX

So now that shuttles are hurtling in the looms of the cotton industry, and white hot cylindrical metal rolls from the furnaces,

And now that buses float on motorways, and the whiplash of tyres approaches the motion which is perfect rest,

And now that a lighthouse keeper senses a black beam forewarning him of greater danger than he himself warns of, and the traffic lights in the 24 hour cities recede into the urban wallpaper,

And now that clowns hang up their wigs and barristers click shut their briefcases,

The genocide and the judge are tried and sentenced, and the emotional relationship between created and creator becomes the impenetrability of silence.

X

For out of the resolution of lecturn-thumping dictators, and the roar of unanimous crowds, and the bootprints in the ashes by Polish crematoria,

For out of the vodka bottles and the rings of polished keys, and the inmates of All the Russias twiddling thumbs on bunks,

For out of half-finished hotels and abandoned concrete-mixers, and neon lettering outfacing a perfect sky,

For out of impoverished musicians and overstuffed ash-trays, and the lonely vomiting in the sink while a bailiff climbs the stairs,

For out of the unimportant citizen hands in pockets wandering the streets, and potplants throwing themselves over balconies jubilant in the sun,

For out of the cadaver and out of the nucleus there comes

The impenetrability of silence.